Electronic Color

Electronic Color

The Art of Color Applied to Graphic Computing

Richard B. Norman, AIA

Professor of Architecture
Clemson University
Clemson, South Carolina

VNR VAN NOSTRAND REINHOLD
New York

Library of Congress Catalog Card Number 89-36261
ISBN 0-442-23539-9

Printed in the United States of America

Van Nostrand Reinhold
115 Fifth Avenue
New York, New York 10003

Van Nostrand Reinhold International Company Limited
11 New Fetter Lane
London EC4P 4EE, England

Van Nostrand Reinhold
480 La Trobe Street
Melbourne, Victoria 3000, Australia

Nelson Canada
1120 Birchmount Road
Scarborough, Ontario M1K 5G4, Canada

16   15   14   13   12   11   10   9   8   7   6   5   4   3   2   1

Library of Congress Cataloging-in-Publication Data

Norman, Richard B., 1933–
   Electronic color: the art of color applied to graphic computing/Richard B.
Norman.
      p.   cm.
   Includes bibliographical references.
   ISBN 0-442-23539-9
   1. Color computer graphics.   I. Title.
T385.N67   1990
006.6—dc20
                                              89-36261
                                              CIP

To Mary, Elizabeth, and Carl

Contents

Foreword

It seems we have reached a seam in knowledge. The progress of human knowledge has been accomplished following one simple principle—learning more and more about less and less. This specialization process has been the way our civilization has moved steadily forward, solved complex problems, and developed remarkable technology. As problems became more complex, we simply divided them into small parts and learned all there is to learn about each part. This condition had developed so naturally that we now know nearly everything about almost nothing. We have reached a seam in knowledge.

The complexity of problems, the size of their fragments, and the depth of our understanding of these fragments have created a demand for a different kind of thinker, a thinker who surveys the plane of knowledge and sees that holes are being dug deeper and deeper into the plane and recognizes that the holes are becoming narrower and narrower as specialization increases. The thinker sees too that people are unable to see out of these narrow deep holes to the other narrow deep holes in the plane; it is becoming more and more difficult to make connections between these holes in the plane of knowledge. This thinker decides to be the connector.

This book was written by this kind of thinker/connector. Its subject is color, which claims a large segment on the plane of knowledge. The book does not dig a narrow, deep hole in one spot on this plane. It asks the reader to dig in several places (computers, aesthetics, history, engineering, art, architecture, perception, urban design) and then it uses color to make the connection. In doing so, it bridges the seam in knowledge.

The book is important for the concepts it documents, and it is also important for the kind of thinking it illustrates, thinking that bridges the seam in knowledge.

Professor Richard Norman's work, thinking, and teaching have been recognized by the American Institute of Architects through the 1988 AIA Education Honor Awards. This award, one of four that year, was given for the innovative and connective qualities found in this book.

James F. Barker, AIA
Dean, College of Architecture
Clemson University
Clemson, South Carolina

Preface

This book is written for the Renaissance person, the individual with dreams to be communicated. For the artist, it offers an introduction to a new technology for the communication of visual ideas; for the scientist, it offers an introduction to principles of art that have existed forever, made simpler to communicate and easier to use because of the new technology.

Thomas Jefferson is admired in the twentieth century as much for the breadth of knowledge he commanded as for his expertise in any particular field. As president, architect, landlord, and scholar, he was able to govern a country and to design buildings. One sometimes hears the phrase "Renaissance man" to describe an individual with a wide range of knowledge and interests. Thomas Jefferson typifies the Renaissance attitude. Today is not a popular time for such people; we admire these individuals, perhaps even envy them a bit, but our educational system and our society rewards the expert more than the generalist.

The age of communication may change this, for computers are making a broad expertise available to everyone. There is a rising demand for individuals with the ability to reassemble knowledge into a coherent whole, to use a broad base of knowledge to convey ideas and information.

If you are an artist, then to be competitive you must learn the technology of the computer in order to present ideas with the forcefulness that computation makes possible. If you are a person of science, then you can master this technology (you probably already have), but you must learn the art of conveying graphic information in order to communicate physical ideas.

Because of computers, the practice of design has been altered; it requires of individuals a broader knowledge base than ever before. With computation we can have at our fingertips all the knowledge that once filled vast libraries, more art than could fill a thousand Louvres, and more technology than was used to put humans on the moon. We can afford to be Renaissance persons.

Computer-aided design is design with color—the monitor of a computer system is a display of interactive color on which design is achieved by color manipulation. If you want to use the capabilities computation provides, then knowledge of color principles will give you control of the computer image, and provide you with a powerful tool for the communication of design ideas. With color graphic computation, the language of color can be spoken with a new forcefulness to communicate information.

Acknowledgments

The majority of the illustrations in this book have been designed on the computer by students of architectural color graphics at the College of Architecture, Clemson University, Clemson, South Carolina. These drawings have been done on the university's VAX cluster of Digital mainframe computers, using Tektronix 4027, 4113, and 4115 terminals. The early work in this course was achieved using software written by Tom Boyer and by Joe Swift of the university computer staff. Later work has made use of DRAFT software, under site license from the architectural firm of Skidmore, Owings & Merrill, Chicago. Photography has been done from terminal screens in the College of Architecture with a Matrix model 3000 color graphic recording camera.

In the College of Architecture I would like to extend thanks to Harlan McClure, James Barker, Lamar Brown, John Jacques, Ken Russo, and Gayland Witherspoon for making both time and equipment available to me and for extending support and assistance when necessary. For their support I would like to thank my colleagues: Bob Hogan, Bob Lowrey, Sandy Elgin, Phyllis Pavorun, and Cathy Robinson. Thanks, too, to my graduate assistants Lance Jaccard and Tim Williams.

I would also like to express appreciation to the following people and acknowledge their assistance:

The members of ACADIA, the Association for Computer Aided Design in Architecture, for their continuing support and encouragement.

The architectural firm of Skidmore, Owings & Merrill, Chicago, for making their software available to the College of Architecture at Clemson, and to Douglas Stoker, Partner in charge of computers at Skidmore, Owings & Merrill, for his encouragement.

The architectural firm of Neal, Prince & Partners, especially Jim Neal and Robin Prince, for their patience and understanding.

Also to Harold Boll, Eikonix; James E. Dalton; Elizabeth English; William J. Mitchell; David Paul Pearson; Doug Smith, WYFF Greenville; Joann M. Taylor, Tektronix; Nicholas Fox Weber, The Josef Albers Foundation; and Stephen Zdepski, School of Architecture, NJIT. I thank them for their encouragement and assistance.

I am particularly indebted to my students, who have diligently persisted in proving that these graphics can be done by computer and whose work appears in this book:

Debra Gardner Beasley
Trey Beatty
Norman E. Bello, Jr.
William J. Blackmon
Steven P. Blisnuk
Todd Boggess
Ana Covington
Renee M. D'Adamo
Stephen M. Denton
Sharon D. Eleazer
Ernest E. Fava, Jr.
Gustus Fischer
Graig A. Gangloff
Charles A. Hardee
Gwinn Gibson Harvey
David A. Hill
Jerry Hupy
Francis R. Irizarri
Lance Jaccard
Robert T. Johnson

G. Scott Kilgore, Sr.
Clifford D. Kinard III
David Owen Loy
William Wesley Lyles
Marc Mascara
Erik Matthews
Scott Murff
Walter Alan Nurmi
David Parker
Richard D. Pittman
Mary C. Read
David Reilly
Matthew Rice
Mark Sangiolo
Peter Schlossman
Amy Kay Stubbs
Peter R. Wehner
Steven A. Wells
Timothy D. Williams
John M. Young, Jr.

Thanks also to the many students whose work could not be included.

Several of the illustrations in this book, academic exercises done by students, illustrate color choices for paintings and for buildings that are assumed to be made by others. Their inclusion here does not imply endorsement by these people of the colors in the illustrations; they are color decisions made by students for comparative purposes and are included to illustrate the computer's ability to compare colors.

Chapter 1

The Language of Color

It might well be argued that color is a universal language, for it transcends the spoken word. Art museums speak a universal tongue through their exhibits. A work of art in a museum communicates through its color, exactly like a computer drawing, though painters have had a thousand years of tradition to build upon, whereas art produced on the computer is new. It is through the display of color that a computer is able to share what previously was communicated only with canvas and paper—an ability to speak the language of color.

The grammar of color is not complicated: color names are one of the first lessons we learn in kindergarten, or in any language course. But the simplicity soon ends, for the use of color as a dynamic means of communication is evasive. Design with color, like design with form, must be learned as any language must be learned, with all its nuances and innuendos, in order to be employed as a powerful means of communication.

TOOLS AND TEACHING

For most people, design is not learned at once, like a revelation; it is a learned subject. Unless one is born into a family with a great awareness of art, design education begins in art class, in grade school, or in high school. There, with a well-directed effort, most individuals are capable of cultivating an ability to produce competent design.

In the American schools of art and architecture design instruction focuses on the studio as the place for drawing and as the center of creative effort. The student discovers the basic elements of design—line, form, space, and color—during the first year in what one might call a traditional design studio. In the studio, projects require these elements to be arranged like building blocks into a series of rudimentary designs (Figure 1.1). From time to time the rational for arranging the blocks changes, driven by current interests in both fashion and

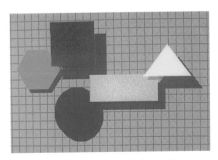

FIGURE 1.1. Composition of squares, circles, and triangles. (Graphic: Steven A. Wells)

philosophy; but while the subject matter may change, the elements remain constant. This basic studio provides an introduction to design and has traditionally been the backbone of both art and architectural pedagogy—the principal method of learning design.

Any design studio depends heavily on tools: pencils, pens, markers, T-squares—whatever media serve best to communicate design ideas. These tools need not be physical; they can also be ideas, attitudes, or processes. Model building was probably the original architectural tool; most buildings completed before and even during the Renaissance in sixteenth-century Europe were designed with models. A few survive, such as the façade models by Michelangelo for the Church of San Lorenzo in Florence. Model building is still common technique and a useful design tool. Models provide a particular way of looking at a design problem. Like building blocks on a nursery floor, the pieces of models submit themselves well to the study of form and space.

Architectural pedagogy changes with the introduction of new tools. During the Renaissance, new techniques for architectural drawing were adapted, culminating in extensive use of the mathematics of perspective as a way of studying the built form. Perspective drawing is a powerful architectural tool, a way to look at buildings that is different from model building—different in technique, but also different in the architecture it produces. The discovery of this tool contributed to the development of baroque architecture in the sixteenth century, and profoundly altered the methodologies of conceptual design.

A pedagogy is shaped by the tools used in teaching. In 1967, Marshall McLuhan wrote: "Societies have always been shaped more by the nature of the media by which men communicate than by the content of the communication" (McLuhan 1967, 8). This is nowhere more true than in the teaching of art and of architecture, where what is taught, what is eventually built, is strongly influenced by the particular tools that are used for its conception. The introduction of tracing paper in the twentieth century changed the way an architect works. With transparent paper it became possible to draw overlays, tracing what was wanted and modifying or adding what was needed. The concept of overlay drawing has now reached fruition with the introduction of computer drawing.

There is turmoil in the teaching of architecture today caused both by the search for new design directions, and by the introduction of computation as a design tool. Teachers are becoming fond of referring to computers as tools. As the computer finds a place in design education, it should become like the triangle, a familiar tool that can be brought out at the proper time to do what it does best. With a tool as complex as the computer, this will not happen overnight. But from both observation and historical perspective, it is suspected that electronic technology is capable of eventually redirecting considerable design effort. According to McLuhan:

> The medium, or process, of our time—electric technology—is reshaping and restructuring patterns of social interdependence and every aspect of our personal life. It is forcing us to reconsider and re-evaluate practically every thought, every action, and every institution formerly taken for granted. (McLuhan 1967, 8)

THE ELEMENTS OF DESIGN

As a drawing tool, computers can draw lines. They may not duplicate the beautiful lines of a well-tempered pencil, but then they have their unique qualities. On the computer it takes some time to organize and draw one line, but if you need a thousand more like it, the computer will outperform the pencil every time (Figure 1.2).

The computer can illustrate space and form. Given the proper software and the underlying mathematical model, a computer can draw perspectives, isometrics, or even orthographic drawings. It contains the mathematical lessons of the Renaissance. Once information is recorded in computer memory, the drawing can become automatic —leaving only the critical decisions to the designer. Used in this way, computation is not providing a new technique, though it can profoundly increase the speed of the drawing process and permit a broader range of observations to be made.

Of the design elements (line, form, space, and color), color has been the most difficult subject to approach in the studio. Who has taken a design studio without experiencing the frustrations of mixing pigments, or of buying colored pencils that were the wrong color when they were applied to a drawing? Until the advent of graphic computation, there has never been an adequate tool in the design studio for the exploration of color as a design element.

Louis Sullivan once said that ornament is *of* the surface and not

FIGURE 1.2. Line drawing on the computer. (Graphic: Walter Alan Nurmi)

on the surface (Sullivan 1947, 189). His ornament was integral to the surface of his buildings; it was usually cast into the stone to become a texture and conceived as a part of the design. What Sullivan accomplished with ornament can also be done with color. One often hears of someone "coloring" a design. Color is an element of the design. It is far richer to design with color than it is to color a design. The computer makes this possible; color is both the joy of the computer and its most difficult challenge. Color graphics require at once a screen of considerable sophistication and a memory capable of storing vast amounts of information. On the screen, we can create an area of color that is at once alive, vibrant, and more important, flexible. If it is too dark we make it lighter, if it is too green we make it more blue. In no way does a computer restrict creative coloration; on the contrary, it encourages exploration. The exhilarating colors of the computer screen can liberate a designer from the restrictions of traditional coloring techniques.

Successful instruction in architectural design should use color graphic computers as an electronic tool in a way that focuses on and uses the strengths and unique capabilities of the instrument. Color as an element of design is a logical focus for a design studio, one that takes advantage of the computer and permits the creative exploration of its full potential. The pursuit of electronic color, as a method of introducing computation to the studio environment, maximizes the unique strengths of this tool. Through its study on the computer, color more easily becomes an element of the design: "Our time is a time for crossing barriers, for erasing old categories—for probing around. When two seemingly disparate elements are imaginatively poised, put in apposition in new and unique ways, startling discoveries often result" (McLuhan 1967, 10). *Color* and *computers* appear to be two such elements.

HOW COLOR SPEAKS

Whether you are working in the structured environment of the design studio or exploring yourself the types of drawing modern computation make available, design can be better understood and more logically practiced using the tools available today. The exercises in this chapter are design studies that utilize color as an approach to design. The principles involved in the exercises are elaborated throughout the book, and will lead you from the simple generation of color designs on a screen into a more complex understanding of the language of color as a design element. They suggest ways in which color can be used to formulate a design, ways in which color can become a part of the design itself.

It is not difficult to do color drawings on a computer. Given a logical software package and an hour or so of instruction, just about anyone can draw color pictures. It is a bit like using the sticker kits that were popular before toys developed their current level of electronic sophistication; simple shapes were pasted together, forming more complex designs. On the computer, you select a shape, decide which color it should be, and paste it on the piece of black paper called the computer screen. For a person who is comfortable in the environment of the design studio, this is both a simple and an enjoyable exercise. It is made more enjoyable on the computer because you are not limited to the supply of polygons—a few triangles, some rectangles, and an assortment of circles—that were available with the old sticker kits.

Shapes can be invented with the computer and their proportions changed as needed. You can make them a little larger or smaller, or even invent your own. The introduction to computation need not be mathematical, technical, or laden with complexity. Turn on your computer. As a beginning task, the creation of a color graphic drawing on the computer can be an exhilarating experience, uninhibited and usually full of the joy of exploration that a new toy can provide. It is a good beginning to design.

Color Contrasts

Computer drawing should begin with pure exploration, with experiencing how colored shapes are made and how they combine. But after an hour or so of such play, stop to look and to see what has been produced (Figure 1.3). Step back and discover that the screen has become a composition of shapes that interact to form a figure-ground pattern. Some shapes appear as a background, some are frontal, depending on the way each color interacts with the adjacent colors. Colors are not usually seen in isolation; they are experienced in relation to other colors, for color is the most relative of the design elements. With a computer, the colors of a composition can be changed easily. Multiple copies of the composition can be made, since computers are excellent at duplicating anything. Alternative color selections

FIGURE 1.3.   Poster design for a school of education. (Graphic: Ana Covington)

could be developed for each copy, resulting in an entirely different color selection for each of several versions of the same composition.

Johannes Itten has said that our perception of a visual image depends on contrast between the various colors that form the image. We experience the world by seeing contrasting colors, the black and white of the printed page or the red and green of a traffic light. The contrasts Itten defined are discussed in Chapter 2. With the computer, it is a simple process to create copies of a drawing and to design a separate color scheme for each copy, and so illustrate the language of a particular contrast. Only the color of the composition need be changed. Figure 1.4 is a modification of a drawing where the colors have been changed to illustrate contrasting *value*. The original composition does not change, though by making a new selection of colors, an entirely new interpretation of the drawing is achieved. Figures 1.5 and 1.6 take this process further by expressing the original composition first in terms of *hue* contrast and then in terms of *saturation* contrast.

How easy this seems. You are able quickly to demonstate the meaning of value, of hue, or of saturation—the three qualities that describe color—and to produce an example of each as a contrasting composition. Without the computer, this is a difficult lesson. It could be done with paint, by carefully mixing each color and applying it to a composition. It could be done with collage, by finding all the color samples and pasting them in place. But these methods provide neither the ease nor the flexibility of the computer. Because of this new tool, we are able to eliminate all other variables and focus on the contribution of color as an element of the design.

FIGURE 1.4.   Contrast of value.
(Graphic: Ana Covington)

FIGURE 1.5.   Contrast of hue.
(Graphic: Ana Covington)

FIGURE 1.6.   Contrast of
saturation. (Graphic: Ana
Covington)

Color Models

We have always named colors, just as we name people. There is much objection now to the omnipresent ID number computers want to attach to people, and probably with good reason. But colors are more impersonal, much more prone to the arithmetic of classification. Names like sky blue, umber, or teal, traditional names given colors, can work against our seeing how different colors relate. If we understand the meaning of *value, hue,* and *saturation* as differing aspects of color, we can define a color model that will organize color just as books are organized in a library. Who, after all, objects to a library giving books a number? A number of these models are discussed in Chapter 3. The properties of color (hue, value, and saturation) can become like axes in a three-dimensional graph: *x, y, z.* A great many color solids have been devised; they are beautiful objects themselves, as are the molecular structure models defined by biologists (Figure 1.7). Collectively, these models illustrate the search for color logic. Individually, they have technical flaws, as do systems for classifying books; but they are capable of giving each color an address so that it can be found as needed.

If you are to work with color, then you must commit a model of the world of color to your mind as a catalog from which to draw your

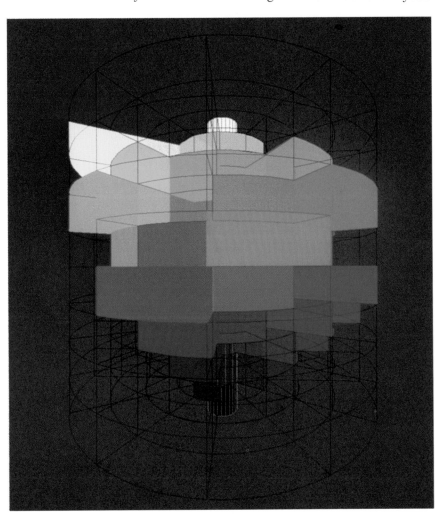

FIGURE 1.7. Computer model of a color solid. (Graphic: Gwinn Gibson Harvey and John M. Young, Jr.)

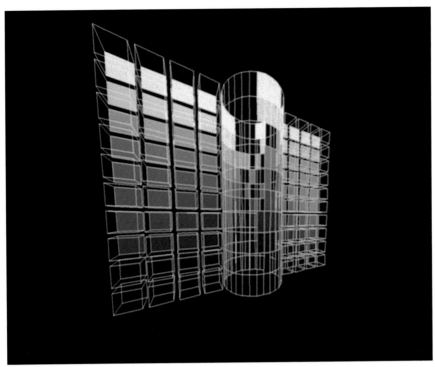

FIGURE 1.8.   Perspective of a color solid. (Graphic: Gregory C. Burchard and Scott Murff)

selections. You must become as familar with each color as the connoisseur is with the varieties of wine. There is no better way to begin this learning than with the exercise of drawing a color model.

Most computer systems have a color solid, either in hardware or in software, that numerically describes a three-dimensional model. The model provides a way to identify a color by numerical definition of the three axes. Figure 1.8 is such a model. It was constructed by students in order to understand the model with which the computer functions. It is a plot of values and of saturations; a vertical axis provides a reference to changing values, with white on top and black on the bottom. Color saturations are increased by moving away from the central pole.

If you take issue with the model incorporated into your equipment, you can define your own color space. As pure mathematics, color models have the potential for being among the more beautiful forms in nature. Munsell, Ostwald, and Gerritsen each have devised a model based on the properties of hue, lightness, and saturation. Each is different in arrangement because it begins with a different presupposition. Figure 1.9 illustrates the section of a color model devised by students based on six primary colors located at the points of a hexagon. There is no better way to appreciate the differences between these colors than to draw them, to select the proper colors with whatever computer system you have, and to locate them properly in a color model. There is no right or wrong to this exercise; color is the most relative of the design elements. We learn to distinguish between colors, as between fine wines, only by knowing how they differ one from another.

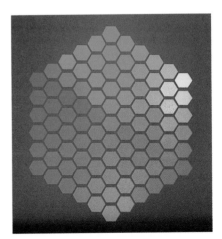

FIGURE 1.9.   Horizontal section through a color solid. (Graphic: Steven P. Blisnuk and Richard Pittman)

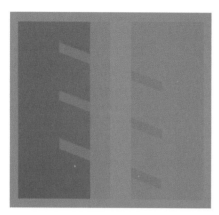

FIGURE 1.10.   One color made to look like two. (Graphic: Jerry Hupy)

The Dynamics of Color

Color has a dynamic quality to it. Like the forces on a railroad bridge that change as a train passes over, a color's appearance is always modified by the colors that surround it. The color studies by Josef Albers discussed in Chapter 5 demonstrate this with clarity and are subject to easy duplication on the computer screen. One color can be made to look like two different colors, or two colors can be made to look like one. What sounds like prestidigitation is not just a demonstration of color magic. Rather, it is a careful illustration of the extent to which environment determines the appearance of a color. Figure 1.10 is a student composition structured on Albers's demonstrations of how one color can be made to appear as two. The diagonal bars in the composition are drawn in one color, though this is realized only by building a mask around them to isolate the color. The act of creating such drawings gives you control of the color palette. You learn to deal with the changing nature of color and gain the ability to select color environments advantagiously.

As an artist, Albers was not averse to mathematics. The sketches for his paintings were meticulous in their numerical definition of proportion (Weber 1988, 238). His color choices, however, would be based on what he saw, rather than on what he could calculate. Color to him was relative, to be analyzed but in the end to be felt and in that way judged good or bad, appropriate or inappropriate. Imagine an object as transparent, he would say, and select a color for the second object when observed through the first (Figure 1.11). By rendering transparency, by placing one object behind another, the illusion of depth is created with color alone. This is how color can be used to define space.

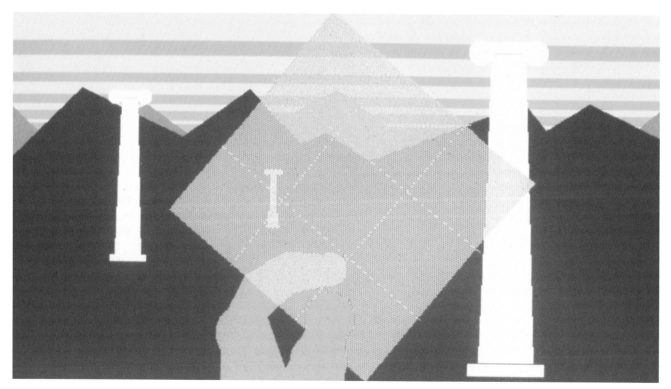

FIGURE 1.11.   Rendering transparency with color. (Graphic: David A. Hill)

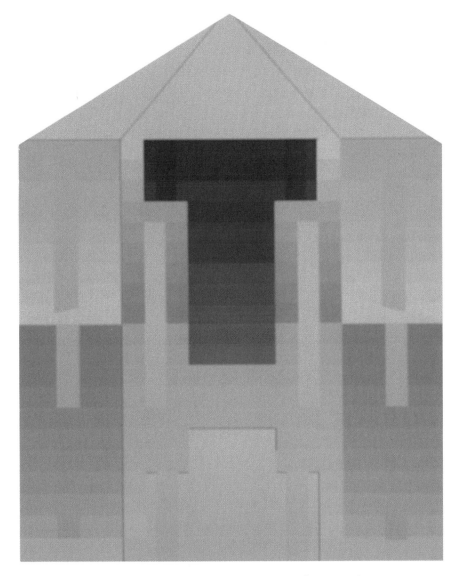

FIGURE 1.12.   Spatial composition in color. (Graphic: David Owen Loy)

The interaction between any two colors is what determines their positions in space. By controlling the relationship between colors, we can determine which colors will be glued together to define the surface of an object, and which will separate in a figure-ground relationship to define a position in space (Figure 1.12). Color is at the heart of visual composition. It is the means by which we visualize the shape, the form, and the arrangement of an architectural composition.

The Relativity of Color

A design relates to its context, to whatever surrounds it; this can be demonstrated on the computer by moving a design element from context to context. With even the most rudimentary display of alternative environments, the relation of an object to its context, of figure to ground, is apparent on the computer screen. Color, being the most relative of the design elements, is particularly sensitive to its environment. If one color is placed on the black of a computer screen, there can be no basis for judgment, good or bad, except for personal color preferences. Two colors on a screen, however, will interact and develop relationships with each other.

Using a computer, a group of colors, a particular color harmony, can be placed in several environments. The colors of an object can be changed to agree with a new environment, while maintaining a constant relationship of the parts to the whole. Figures 1.13 and 1.14 illustrate alternative color schemes for a house, providing a tool for exploring alternatives as a basis for color decisions. What can be done with architecture can be done with art. Figures 1.15 and 1.16, based on a painting by Andy Warhol, use color alternatives to explore hair colors for Marilyn Monroe.

There is nothing unique about these changes of color, no new magic that is electronically generated. They are exercises that have always been possible, though now the speed of electronics makes it feasible to explore variations creatively, to experience color and how it affects the form of a design.

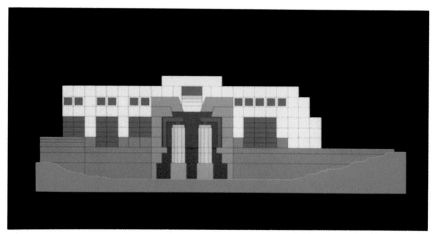

FIGURE 1.13.   Computer illustration of the Plocek House by Michael Graves. (Graphic: David Owen Loy)

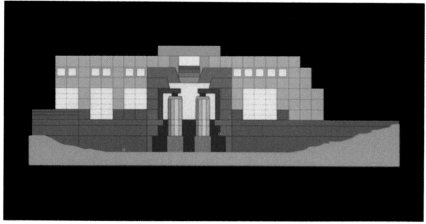

FIGURE 1.14.   Alternative color selections for the Plocek House. (Graphic: David Owen Loy)

ELECTRONIC COLOR AS TEACHER

With the introduction of electronic media into the design studio, the manipulation of color as a design element becomes feasible. The practice of designing and then coloring can end, although old habits need to be broken. As long as the computer is seen as a line drawing tool, we will continue to color designs that have been conceived as linear compositions. By recognizing the computer screen as a field of color, we can direct attention to the effects of one color on another. We can use color as an essential element of the design—as the substance of architectural form.

These exercises could form a syllabus for the introduction of color to the studio. But in fact they are capable of transcending that syllabus; they go beyond introducing a new tool and developing appropriate studio applications. What begins as a reaction to a new tool produces a result that would not have been possible before the computer, or at best would have been difficult. By pursuing the strengths of computation, we develop a new avenue for creative expression.

In the design studio, the pursuit of color as an element of design will be strengthened by using the computer. There need be no apology for what is displayed; forceful new images can be created. This powerful new way to look at design parallels our own visual experiences. As at the beginning of perspective drawing, we will see the old familiar world once again—through a new pair of glasses.

FIGURE 1.15. Marilyn Monroe, adapted on the computer from a painting by Andy Warhol. (Graphic: Francis R. Irizarri)

EXERCISES

1. On the computer, do a composition that is composed of areas of color. Work for an interesting figure-ground pattern. No line work should be used.
2. Use the computer to create a copy of your drawing, and then modify the colors of the copy to illustrate hue, value, or saturation contrast.
3. Explore the colors your computer can create. Are there choices? Can you draw a diagram of the color solid you will be using?

REFERENCES

Albers, Joseph. 1963. *Interaction of Color.* New Haven, CT: Yale University Press.

Itten, Johannes. 1973 [1961]. *The Art of Color: The Subjective Experience and Objective Rationale of Color.* Trans. Ernst van Haagen. New York: Van Nostrand Reinhold.

McLuhan, Marshall. 1967. *The Medium Is the Massage.* New York: Bantam Books.

Sullivan, Louis H. 1947. Ornament in architecture. In *Kindergarten Chats (revised 1918) and Other Writings.* Originally published in *The Engineering Magazine,* August 1892.

Weber, Nicholas Fox. 1988. The artist as alchemist. In *Josef Albers: A Retrospective.* New York: Solomon R. Guggenheim Museum.

FIGURE 1.16. Alternative color selections. (Graphic: Francis R. Irizarri)

Chapter 2

A Theory of Contrasts

T he time between the two world wars was a period of critical thought on the continent of Europe, a time that gave rise to theories and to methods of teaching that would revolutionize both art and architectural education. In the world of art, the age of impressionism had passed and the work of a new generation that had been interrupted by World War I was beginning anew. In Germany this was the era of the Bauhaus, and of a questioning of the precepts of art and architecture that were fostered by its leaders.

THE BAUHAUS

Opened in Weimar, Germany, in 1919 and later moved to Dessau, the Bauhaus was founded upon the ashes of World War I. It thrived in the aftermath of war, having been born of the desperation and nurtured by the hope that was the Weimar Republic of postwar Germany. Both institutions, the Bauhaus and the republic, were destined to last a critical fourteen years. The Bauhaus fought to exist in the rampant inflation that consumed the republic around it. It drew a younger generation of artists from all over Europe and bound them together to redefine education in the arts and crafts. It was closed in 1933 by Adolf Hitler as the first tangible expression of his new Nazi government's cultural policy (Whitford 1984, 9).

The founder and first director of the Bauhaus was Walter Gropius, an architect, who was given the task of melding the fine arts and the craft traditions of Europe into a new institution. This school was to be supportive of both the industrial revolution and the German industrial base, which the Weimar Republic was attempting to rebuild. The Bauhaus came into being on the premise that all the arts existed in a state of isolation from which they could be rescued and given common directions and goals. Trained in a cooperative environment, painters, sculptors, and craftsmen were to combine their artistic skills in order to achieve a greater art (Whitford 1984, 11).

From the beginning of the school, Gropius insisted on a system of team teaching—workshops, rather than studios, as the basis of instruction. These workshops were to be directed by *workshop masters*, master craftsmen who would instruct apprentices in their particular craft. It was Gropius's idea that the shops would become far more than craft studios; each workshop was to be taught by both a *workshop master* and a *master of form*. The latter was an artist carefully chosen by Gropius and charged with the mission of introducing students to the "mysteries of creativity and help(ing) them achieve a formal language of their own" (Whitford 1984, 30). It was fondly hoped that an integration of the arts and crafts could be achieved through this partnership.

One of the first masters of form was Johannes Itten, a Swiss-born painter who came to the Bauhaus already familiar with the work of such European educational reformers as Froebel and Montessori. At Itten's insistence, the four-year curriculum at the Bauhaus began with a *Vorkurs*—a first year of study that was common to all workshops. The idea that there could be a first-year core curriculum for all the arts, common in schools of art and architecture today, is based on Itten's development of the *Vorkurs*.

The arrival of Johannes Itten brought to the Bauhaus a person of extraordinary interests and ideas, an individual who was destined to become a virtual cult figure at the school. His physical appearance was extraordinary: Itten's head was shorn of hair, and he wore clothes of his own design that ran contrary to any sense of current style. Both his personality and his personal beliefs could be described as bizarre and tended for years to overshadow his teachings of both the fundamentals of art and the behavior of color.

Itten was a Mazdaznan, a member of an early twentieth-century religious sect whose beliefs were related to the teachings of Zoroaster and to the beliefs of modern Indian Parsees (Whitford 1984, 51). This combination of religious zeal and dedicated teaching produced a focused attitude and made the theories he taught a virtual cause with which students were expected to align themselves. Zoroastrians saw the world as a battlefield between good and evil, between black and white. From his own iron-willed attitude of left and right, of contrasting ideas, Itten developed philosophies that permeated both his teaching and the lifestyle of his students. An awareness of life through art was to be found in a series of contrasting elements. According to Itten, "All perception takes place in terms of contrasts: nothing can be seen on its own, independent from something else of different quality" (Whitford 1984, 55).

In the *Vorkurs* of the Bauhaus, Johannes Itten developed what he called "an aesthetic color theory originating in the experience and intuition of a painter" (Itten 1973, 11). In his definitive work *The Art of Color*, Itten explores both the history and the science of color, relating all of this to his experiences as teacher and painter. He proposes that all visual perception is the result of seven specific methods of color contrast. As he explains them: "Each is unique in character and artistic value, in visual, expressive and symbolic effect, and together they constitute the fundamental resource of color design" (Itten 1973, 36).

THE SEVEN CONTRASTS OF JOHANNES ITTEN

The color contrasts identified by Johannes Itten can provide an excellent starting point for the study of color on the computer. We examine the contrasts here in terms of their ability to affect design; they are explored in a historic context through painting, and in a modern sense through their application to computer graphics. Together these contrasts offer a fundamental vocabulary for the design of color graphics on the computer; whether they may be successfully applied to architecture through computation remains a challenge to architects and to those who devise the computers they use.

The classic paintings of the French impressionists provide outstanding examples of most of these contrasts; there is a correlation between the techniques of the impressionist painter and those of the computer graphic designer. As a movement in art, impressionism was particularly conscious of the effects of color in conveying a graphic message and so provides excellent illustrative material for these contrasts. The illustrations in this chapter are selected from among many examples of impressionist works, both those of the French masters and those produced by artists in the American South. Although less well known than the European impressionists, the inventive use of color by these American artists invites a fresh examination of how color is capable of speaking to either the graphic artist or the electronic colorist.

Contrast of Value

The contrast of black and white, of lightness and darkness, is the most fundamental of the visual contrasts. We have no trouble understanding both the meaning and the emotion conveyed by a black and white picture. In the darkroom of an early nickelodeon theater, sights never before seen by human eyes unfolded in black and white before astonished audiences. There was no sound and no chroma in the early movies, but who in even today's technicolor world could resist laughing at the tribulations of W. C. Fields or the endless frustrations of Charlie Chaplin? A similar drama took place in the late 1940s as television made its debut in the American home. TV sets had postage stamp screens, the biggest of them perhaps smaller than the book you are holding, but the drama they presented captured the imagination of a generation of people, providing instantaneous acceptance of a new means of communication. While technicolor has added considerable sparkle to the movies, and while color in television has added appreciably to the enjoyment of home entertainment systems, it would be difficult to argue that the introduction of color has increased understanding of the content of either film or television beyond the simple value contrasts of their black and white predecessors.

We have come to accept the power of a black and white image. What would television be, what acceptance would the nickelodeon images have found, if their black and white images had been reduced to line drawings, to wire-frame images? Would photographic images presented as line drawings have found the acceptance that greeted the black and white pictures on television or in the movies? If today's computer images were built with the contrasting grays of black and white imagery (Figure 2.1) rather than with the stick figures of wire-frame construction (Figure 2.2), would they not find greater acceptance in the world of art and architecture? The reduction of a color picture to its component areas of contrasting value is an abstraction we are readily able to accept; its reduction to a line drawing is considerably less acceptable.

The contrast of value is fundamentally the contrast between black and white. More specifically, it is a series of contrasts that are possible between the stages of gray as they are arrayed between the poles of black and white. One can make a chart of this with a series of color samples. White is on the top, black on the bottom. Between them are arrayed all the neutral gray color samples one can imagine, with the lighter samples toward white and the darker ones toward black. Although it is an infinite series of color variation, in fact the eye can discern only twenty steps with ease, perhaps forty steps with young eyes and a good visual education. These forty grays comprise the palette of all black and white presentations. They are a graphic language we all understand.

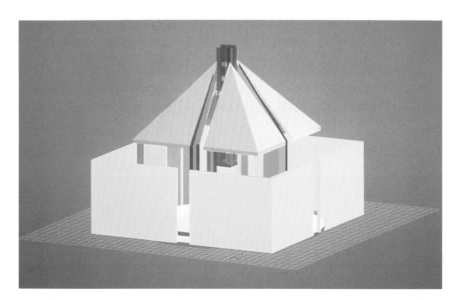

FIGURE 2.1.   Computer drawing using color. (Graphic: Erik Matthews)

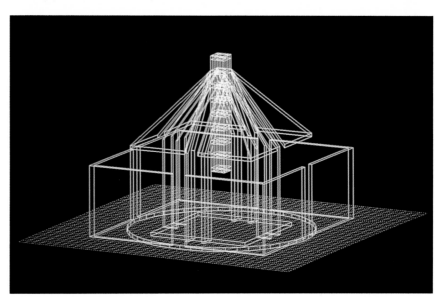

FIGURE 2.2.   Wire-frame computer drawing. (Graphic: Erik Matthews)

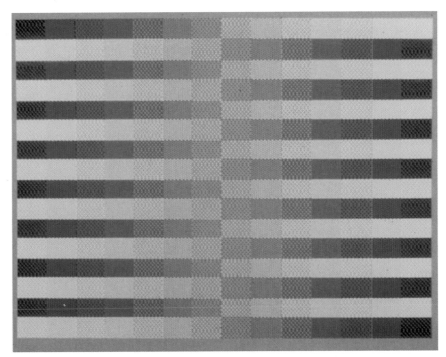

FIGURE 2.3.   Contrast in gray, computer adaptation of Albers 1963.
(Graphic: Peter Schlossman)

A scale of grays in twenty parts, perhaps more, perhaps less, can be easily or even mathematically achieved on the computer. But one must be careful with such mathematics, for it often relates more to the technology of a particular computer than to the rules of perception. A scale of gray values should contain equal visual steps between each color. There should be no perceived line between two samples where the eye moves quickly from light to dark; you should experience the visual continuum from white to black. In building such a scale on the computer, you must beware of "instruction book logic"; let your eye be your guide. If color could really be measured and defined analytically, then the world would be both a lot simpler and a lot duller.

Through Itten's careful instruction, his students cultivated an ability to write "music" with the gray scales. It takes only four or five colors. Most of us could play Beethoven's Fifth on a piano with only four strokes of a finger, or "Mary Had a Little Lamb" with seven. How many colors are needed to play a song on the gray scale? Not too many, and on a computer they are quick and simple compositions. But we soon discover that while the technology of a gray scale composition is simple, this is a difficult assignment. The variables of a black and white composition are many. Each drawing will develop a figure-background relationship as the areas of gray are manipulated to make some objects frontal, some background (Figure 2.3). A vocabulary of basic design principles can very quickly be brought into a discussion of black and white drawings, even though gray is the only color involved.

Paintings often depend on the contrast of black and white elements in order to communicate. They need not be strictly black and white compositions, nor even in values of gray, for the value differences that are to be found within a particular hue can be equally

FIGURE 2.4. Composition in contrasting values. (Graphic: Robert T. Johnson)

effective in conveying a graphic message (Figure 2.4). Yet the essential contrast, the communication of content that any composition affords, is usually achievable through the contrast of value.

Savannah Nocturne is a view of the Savannah riverfront in Georgia, painted at sunset (Figure 2.5). It shows how value contrast can forcefully communicate both form and mood. The light of the river reflects both the last rays of sunlight and the lights from the far shore, contrasting with the sail of the ship and the dark of a disappearing land mass. It is like a sepia photograph, illuminated by a strong source of light and sculpted by the darkness of the surrounding form.

Figure 2.6 shows a student composition, drawn on the computer, that makes use of the same principle. The cube, in perspective, is only given enough value to articulate its mass. All attention is drawn to the circular opening in its base, which—like the river in the Savannah painting—is illuminated with a much lighter color. Both compositions create a focus and establish a mood by this use of contrasting value.

Contrast of value in a painting can be subtle and yet still be effective. Figure 2.7 is a computer adaptation of a painting by Picasso, drawn on the computer as a study of value contrasts. The drawing is about a guitar, although it never appears as an object. The parts suggesting a guitar are identified by their light value. The movement and effectiveness of this painting are strongly reinforced by value contrasts. Neither black nor white nor gray appear in this composition, but by selecting colors to form a contrast of value, the painting communicates its central theme (Itten 1973, 62).

FIGURE 2.5.   Eliot Clark, *Savannah Nocturne*. 1925. Oil on canvas.
(Courtesy of Kennedy Galleries, Inc., New York)

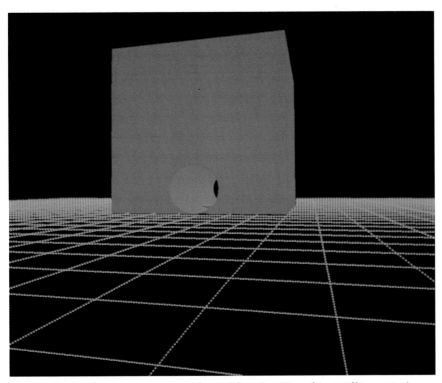

FIGURE 2.6.   Computer composition with cube. (Graphic: William Wesley
Lyles)

FIGURE 2.7.   Computer adaptation of a painting by Pablo Picasso. (Graphic: Ernest E. Fava, Jr.)

Explorations in the use of contrasting value are an excellent introduction to electronic color. Such compositions need not be dependent on extensive color capabilities, for ways can be found to draw a scale of grays on even the simplest computer. Once the piano of color notes is invented, it can be played, with compositions simple or complex, to express the essence of a design. Ideas can be communicated using solid areas of color with a strength that is difficult to achieve in line drawing, even if the colors are but shades of gray. Technically, on a computer, no more is involved than turning on or off the phosphors that illuminate the screen.

Contrast of Hue

The idea of color is usually associated with the hue of an object. *Hue* can be defined as that quality that distinguishes one color from another, which distinguishes redness from blueness or yellowness from greenness. For the painter, hue is the pure substance of a pigment; to the scientist, it is light of a particular wavelength, a part of the visible spectrum discussed in Chapter 3.

Hue adds diversity to the world; it contributes to its richness and to the uniqueness of every object in it. In its simplest form, *contrast of hue* is a self-evident concept: we drive or stop our cars based on the contrast of red and green. As black and white are the extremes in value contrast, so red and green represent extremes in the contrast of hue. When we set up a color code to identify the pipes in a boiler room, we would not use values, for they are too relative. Instead we use hues; hot water pipes are red and cold water pipes, blue. Within our culture, this is a comprehensible code that needs no guidebook or comparison. It draws strength from the unique qualities of red or of blue to distinguish one item from another.

Contrast of hue is the simplest of contrasts to comprehend, a fact that probably accounts for its frequent and recurring use in primitive art and in folk art everywhere. In Itten's words: "The undiluted primaries and secondaries always have a character of aboriginal cosmic splendor as well as of concrete actuality. Therefore they serve equally well to portray a celestial coronation or a mundane still life" (Itten 1973, 37).

The Dutch painter Piet Mondrian spent the latter part of his life producing a series of abstract paintings in a manner that typified the attitudes of the Bauhaus. His paintings are based on two contrasts: of hue and of size. He used only five pigments: red, yellow, and blue—the three primary colors advocated by the Bauhaus—plus black and white. Each color was used only in its pure form. Ultimately Mondrian eliminated diagonal lines from his work and placed pigments in an orthographic grid in order to explore compositional attitudes that would exploit the qualities of the individual hues. As a colorist, Mondrian accepted the primary colors in their rudimentary state and used them to explore the potential of hue contrast as a pictorial concept.

In Figure 2.8 a painting by Mondrian has been copied on the computer. Here all five colors of his palette are present in a balanced composition, the visual weight of each hue being carefully considered in order to reduce compositional elements to a minimum. The simple geometry of Mondrian's work submits well to computer analysis; hav-

FIGURE 2.8.   Computer adaptation of a painting by Piet Mondrian, *Tableau II*. (Graphic: Mark Sangiolo)

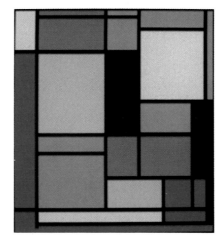

FIGURE 2.9.   Computer modifications to *Tableau II*, pastel hues. (Graphic: Mark Sangiolo)

FIGURE 2.10.   Computer modifications to *Tableau II*, strong hues. (Graphic: Mark Sangiolo)

FIGURE 2.11.   Computer modifications to *Tableau II*, black to gray. (Graphic: Mark Sangiolo)

ing copied both color and composition, the colors can be decomposed electronically. By working with color changes, the contribution of color as a compositional element in the painting can be explored. In Figure 2.9 the strong primary hues have been removed and replaced with an assortment of soft pastels. Immediately the composition changes; the careful balance that existed in the original painting is destroyed, and the mood has been altered. Figure 2.10 develops a very different palette of hues; here the magentas and peachlike tones that are introduced again alter both composition and meaning. Finally, in Figure 2.11, the black grid of the composition is changed to gray. The graphic designer has taken extraordinary liberties with these color changes. Ultimately the spirit of the drawing owes very little to Mondrian, yet the composition is unchanged; all that has been done is to manipulate the hue contrasts that were present in the original painting.

On a simple color monitor, contrast of hue is about the only option available to the designer, for a rudimentary electronic palette of six-

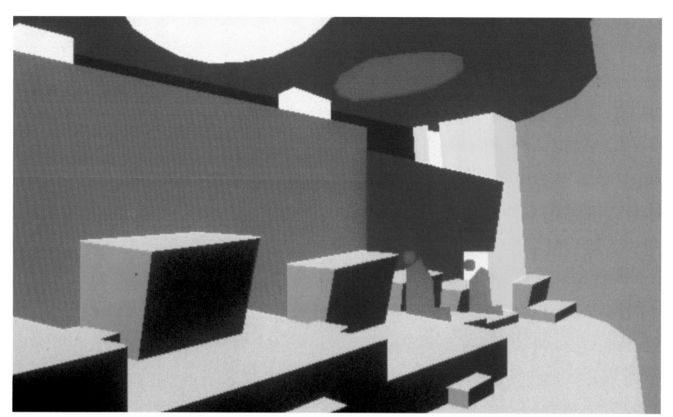

FIGURE 2.12.   Computer rendering of chapels by Le Corbusier at La Tourette. (Graphic: David A. Hill)

teen colors allows few choices. Considerable design work can be achieved, however, using color in order to improve the business graphics that such computer equipment is designed to produce. A well-colored graph can convey several levels of meaning beyond the raw data it is designed to illustrate. Hues appropriate to the subjects illustrated can be selected and combined in ways that are appealing, or perhaps upsetting, if that is the intent of the graph. Meaning can be suggested with the proper selection and combination of hues. Colors can be manipulated, just as the simple compositions of Mondrian can be changed, to suggest a variety of moods. The psychology of these changes is discussed in Chapter 7.

The architect and painter Le Corbusier made extraordinary use of hue contrast in the design of buildings. Using just primary colors, he was able to color large areas effectively. Figure 2.12 is a computer drawing of three chapels in the monastery at La Tourette. The rooms, intended as settings for the private celebration of Mass, were each identified with a primary color. The effectiveness of the original hue selections as a part of the design is made clear in Figure 2.13, where the graphic designer has explored modifications. Through change of hue contrast, the intent of the original design has been lost and the color becomes only decorative.

Matthias Grünewald, painting two hundred years before Newton, postulated the fundamentals of color organization and made extensive use of the natural circuit of hues (see Chapter 3). His Isenheim Altarpiece includes illustrations of biblical stories that were drawn using

FIGURE 2.13.   Computer modification to the colors of Le Corbusier's chapels. (Graphic: David A. Hill)

hue contrast to explore the spectrum. The *Resurrection and Transfiguration of Jesus* (Figure 2.14) makes use of a progression of colors from the whiteness of the shroud on the central figure, through blue, purple, violet, red, orange, and yellow, returning to the white figure of Christ. Grünewald uses the gamut of colors in logical progression to develop contrasts between hues. This progression is used to give form, substance, and importance to the Christ figure in the painting. Grünewald recognized that each hue has, in its saturated state, a natural value. His use of these values is strong and assertive. But the motivating force of the painting is achieved through the use of contrasting hue. Taking advantage of hue contrasts, Grünewald separates natural phenomena from the supernatural, giving earthly colors to the guards and presenting the heavenly figure in a robe of color that achieves, through hue selection, a distinction apart from worldly affairs (Itten 1973, 142).

The extraordinary palette of color with which we design today provides, both in art and in architecture, ample opportunity to use the full intensity of hue contrast. It is worth noting that Grünewald has placed all this color in probably 10 percent of the visual environment. The painting was intended as the focal point of an enormous gray church. In the whole of the church there is only one shroud, one Christ rising from amid a vast environment of subdued hue. Grünewald, like Mondrian, makes use of contrasting size as well as hue. To be successful, the design of a graphic composition must consider the intended use, for contrast with its setting is as important to a success-

FIGURE 2.14.   Matthias Grünewald, *Resurrection and Transfiguration of Jesus.* From the Isenheim altarpiece, 1475–1528. Colmar, Unterlinden Museum. (Courtesy of Giraudon/Art Resource, New York)

ful composition as is the internal contrast. For example, on entering the Church of Santa Croce in Florence today and seeing the crucified Christ of Cimabue hanging at the crossing, we are confronted with an experience similar to what Grünewald intended. With this one dramatic gesture of proportion and contrasting hue, the painter has made a deeply religious statement.

Contrast of hue is a powerful design element whose power must be nurtured and used at the right moment or it can be lost. Within each hue are associations that go beyond what can be communicated in gray. The psychology of these associations is discussed in Chapter 7.

Contrast of Saturation

A color is fully saturated when it is at its maximum brilliance. Though often confused with value, saturation is a very different quality of color, and its use as a contrasting element produces a very different effect. Figure 2.15 shows the same composition as in Figure 2.4, but modified to illustrate contrasting saturations. Any color, any hue, has a low saturation when it approaches gray in color. Conversely, saturation is high when the coloring element is most pure. In dealing with pigment, color can be lightened or darkened through mixing to produce a change in value. Color may also be reduced in saturation

FIGURE 2.15.   Composition with contrasting saturations. (Graphic: Robert T. Johnson)

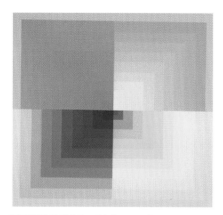

FIGURE 2.16. Value and saturation contrasts. (Graphic: David Owen Loy)

through mixing, bringing it closer to a neutral gray. Fully saturated color cannot be created by mixing; it is an intense, vivid color that comes from a color source. Though saturated hues are not usually seen in nature, they appear occasionally as the bloom of a flower. Maximum saturation can be found in pure paint pigment or in the phosphors that produce the colored light in a computer terminal. It is probably good advice to use fully saturated color sparingly, for like the frosting on a cake, one soon has enough of it.

Color saturation cannot be increased through mixing, because the mixture of two colors is always lower in saturation than either of the source colors. The history of painting is in part a history of the search for more vividly saturated pigments. Fruits, berries, and soils, natural substances that were the sources of early pigmentation, do not yield high saturation. The synthetic colorants developed in the nineteenth and early twentieth centuries provide all the arts with media of far more intense saturation than was previously available. Color in the twentieth century has become much more saturated due to the development of these chemical pigment sources.

The phenomena of saturation contrast and that of value contrast are not easily separated, though they are totally different qualities of color. Yellow, fully saturated yellow, is a very light hue; it is a brilliant color that we often think of as representing light. It cannot be made darker without desaturating the color. There is no "brilliant" dark yellow. Likewise, a fully saturated blue is by nature a very dark value. It cannot be lightened without losing its saturation. Each hue has a value at which it is most brilliant—at which its most saturated form is displayed. This is immutable: It is not awaiting the invention of some new dyestuff; it is an ingrained quality of the particular hue, a part of the nature of the color.

In developing a graphic composition or in resolving architectural colors, control of both value and saturation is paramount to successful coloration. A room, a building, or a painting may be colored in blue or red or green; the ultimate selection is largely an issue that ties together taste, fashion, and psychology and will be discussed further in Chapter 7. It is the selection of value and of saturation that determines the final composition. Figure 2.16 is a composition that uses both contrasts, contrast of saturation on the top and contrast of value on the bottom. The difference is clear; each contrast is a potent element of color, an element to be contrasted and composed—to be used as the substance of the work of art.

It is a difficult feat to develop a painting based on contrast of saturation alone. Although often combined with the lightness and darkness of contrasting values, the use of saturation contrasts can add much to the effectiveness of a painting. Gari Melchers, in a painting titled *Snow* (Figure 2.17), has used a very close range of hues, from purple-blue to magenta. Value contrasts, except for the frame of the window, are minimal. But the high saturation he uses in coloring the central figure, her skin tones and her dress, contrasts sharply with the low saturation of the city seen through the window. The effectiveness of the picture is achieved through this use of contrasting saturation.

Saturation on the computer is achieved from the phosphors that form the color image. Red, green, and blue, the phosphor colors, display the highest possible saturation. Mixing them can only reduce their intensity. For example, if we want a fully saturated yellow, regardless of the method of color selection we choose to use, on the computer terminal we will see yellow by displaying the red and green phosphors at the same time. It will be brilliant, a yellow of the maximum achievable saturation. But as a mixture it will not have the brilliance—the saturation—of either red or green. Any color wheel drawn on the computer will show its greatest level of saturation when using a maximum amount of the color source, unless this has been understood and a compensation made. (Figure 3.14 shows such a wheel.) Occasionally it is necessary to gray the hues of the source in order that they may be equal in saturation to their adjacent hues.

FIGURE 2.17.   Gari Melchers. *Snow*, 1921, oil on canvas, 43″ × 31⅛″, Belmont, The Gari Melchers Memorial Gallery, Mary Washington College, Fredericksburg, Virginia.

FIGURE 2.18. Contrast of hue.
(Graphic: Timothy D. Williams)

The subtle as well as the obvious points of difference between value and saturation are not easily demonstrated using paints. On a computer screen, the differences can be seen quickly and dramatically by adjusting the percentages of each factor. Figures 2.18, 2.19, and 2.20 illustrate the differences between value, hue, and saturation. Although each figure is the same composition, the colors have been modified in order to develop a separate composition for each of the three contrasts.

In articulating the contrasts of value, hue, and saturation, Johannes Itten has defined the three elements that are at the basis of human color perception. They are the basis of most color models and offer a clue to the organization of color, as we will see in Chapter 3. To complete his image of the nature of perception, Itten defined four additional contrasts.

Cold–Warm Contrast

If you enjoy swimming, then you already have a good understanding of the *cold–warm contrast*. A lake can feel very cold in the heat of the day, but if you return at midnight when the air has chilled, the same water will feel much warmer; there is a warmth to the midnight water that could not be found at noon because of the heat of the sun. Cold–warm contrast is an experience to which we are constantly exposed as we move from heated, to cooled, to natural environments. It is always a relative experience.

FIGURE 2.19. Contrast of value. (Graphic: Timothy D. Williams)

FIGURE 2.20. Contrast of saturation. (Graphic: Timothy D. Williams)

FIGURE 2.21.   William P. Silva, *Magic Pool.* 1924, oil on canvas, 34″ × 39″.
(Courtesy of The Fine Arts Center, Cheekwood, Nashville, TN)

This same contrast can be found in color, for every color is perceived as having a temperature. It is no accident that hot pipes are colored red and cold pipes colored blue. Red is warmer than blue. It has been proven that a room painted red feels warmer than a room painted blue. But color temperature, like water temperature, is relative. A color may be warm in contrast to one color, but cool in contrast to another.

The contrast between cold and warm is critical to the perception of depth. The color of a surface in sunlight is warmer than the same surface color seen in shade. The layering of sunlight and shade, of warm and cool, creates steps in the field of vision that are perceived as depth. A scenario can be built into a graphic composition by looking through a dark frame into a field of sunlight, and then into the shadows beyond. To the casual observer, there is very little depth in the landscape of the American Southwest; the continuous warm tone of the desert floor leads the eye a mile, maybe five miles, to a distant mesa. It is not like the warm meadow seen through the cool shadows of trees. In drawing architectural perspectives, we are usually advised to place an object in the foreground in order to give depth to the picture. In terms of color, the foreground is, more often than not, drawn in shadow in order to contrast with the warm, sunlit tones of the building being illustrated.

The layering of cold–warm contrast can be seen in Figure 2.21, a painting by William P. Silva, where the cool blue-green tones of the foreground give way first to the warm cyan of the water, then to the warmer yellow and green of grass and trees. In the far distance an area of cool blue-magenta adds yet another layer of depth to the landscape.

This principle can also be applied to the design of buildings. Architects lead people through a series of spaces that are made interesting by their spatial contrasts. As the coloration is developed for spaces, they can distinguish themselves by size or by temperature: It is always a pleasure to move from a cold hallway into a room filled with sun.

Figure 2.22 is a computer drawing adapted from Henri Matisse's *Madame Matisse*, known also as The Green Line. The line runs down the center of her face, dividing this portrait between warm and cool. There is no shadowing to be seen, only the selection of color to determine a light source and to model the surface of the face. To balance the portrait, the warmer portion of her face is seen against a cool background; the cool side is backed by warm colors. To prove the validity of the cool–warm contrast, the colors have been altered by computer, first to create a warm portrait (Figure 2.23) and then a cooler version (Figure 2.24). It should be clear that neither of these colorations provide the pictorial interest of the original.

Using the same manipulation of cold–warm contrast demonstrated in the Matisse painting, the portrait of Michelangelo's *David* shown in Figure 2.25 is sculpted by computer using only the warmth of magenta and the coolness of green; the portrait is achieved with cold–warm contrast alone.

One must be careful to discern between cold–warm contrast and contrast of value. While they often go hand in hand, emotionally and physically they are quite different. Properly used, cold–warm contrast is capable of having a profound effect on the mood of a painting, a building, or a graphic design.

FIGURE 2.22. Computer adaptation of Matisse, *Madame Matisse—The Green Line*. (Graphic: Debra Gardner Beasley)

FIGURE 2.23. *The Green Line* in warm colors. (Graphic: Debra Gardner Beasley)

FIGURE 2.24. *The Green Line* in cool colors. (Graphic: Debra Gardner Beasley)

FIGURE 2.25.   *David.* (Graphic: David Parker)

Complementary Contrast

Warm and cool colors appear on opposite sides of the color wheel. When they are exact opposites, they are called *complementary colors.* There are many such pairs—in fact, an infinite number of pairs arranged around the circuit of hues. If the colors are true complements, truly opposite colors, then they combine to neutralize each other and form a gray. This can be proved by using the computer to draw a simple checkerboard of color. If the colors used are complements, pure red and pure cyan for example, they will be perceived as gray when seen from a distance. If the scale of the checkerboard is sufficiently small, this gray will be apparent at arm's length; but if the board is sized for a game of checkers, you may have to back up across the room in order to see the gray. When the scale of color sample becomes small enough so that the field is seen as one color, the mixture appears as gray. This provides a good test of whether two colors are actually complementary.

The definition of colors as complementary and the visual effect that can be achieved by their use as complements is different from the effect of using a cold–warm contrast. When the scale of mixture is small, complementary colors will effectively cancel each other; but when the scale is sufficiently large to see individual colors, they intensify each other to their greatest brilliance. More often than not, the squares of a real checkerboard form a complementary contrast, the better to distinguish one square from the other. As Itten describes them: "Two such colors make a strange pair. They are opposite, they require each other. They incite each other to maximum vividness when adjacent; and they annihilate each other, to gray-black, when mixed—like fire and water" (Itten 1973, 78).

The eye seems to require a balance of complements. The use of complements is a common and often repeated method of color harmony in interior design; probably it is the best understood of all color principles. Faced with a problem in color selection, you are well advised to begin your search for harmony by turning to complementary contrast, though many a freshman color scheme has been devastated by an overdose of fully saturated complements. But used well, the power of one color to demand another becomes a forceful design tool.

Look again at the impressionist work done in the American South. Gilbert Gaul's *Picking Cotton* (Figure 2.26) illustrates how the choice of a complementary color selection can bring balance and harmony to a painting. Here the red clay soil of the South is countered with the green of the cotton fields; the sky repeats the red in a lower saturation; one blouse, done in a brighter red, focuses the eye on the central character. The color of both crop and soil is intensified by the selection of complements.

FIGURE 2.26.   Gilbert Gaul, *Picking Cotton*. ca. 1890. Oil on canvas, 13¼″ × 18¼″. (In the collection of The Corcoran Gallery of Art; museum purchase through the gift of Josephine B. Crane)

FIGURE 2.27.   Henri de Toulouse-Lautrec, *At the Moulin Rouge.* 1892, oil on canvas, 123.0 × 141.0 cm, Helen Birch Bartlett Memorial Collection, 1928.610. (©1989 The Art Institute of Chicago. All rights reserved.)

FIGURE 2.28.   Chinese temple. (Graphic: Mary C. Read)

The French impressionist painters made good use of complementary color balance. Henri Toulouse-Lautrec's characters in *At the Moulin Rouge* (Figure 2.27) derive their qualities as much from the painter's choice of color as from their own personalities. The painting is a composition in red and green. Without stretching a point too far, one could describe the "good guys" as red and the "bad guys" as green, somewhat like the black and white costumes of villains and heroes in an old melodrama. The green face at the right-hand edge (made greener by the red, red lips) is an eerie character, a gaslit dancer a world apart from the red-haired patron at the table. Wherever an edge needs emphasis in the painting, it seems to find its complement.

The Chinese temple in Figure 2.28 uses a simple balance of red-green complements to form the architecture. There is a comfortable color relationship, using some of the traditional colors of China.

Simultaneous Contrast

Sometimes the complement for a color is not to be found in a composition. In this case the situation is set for the most mysterious of color phenomena, *simultaneous contrast*. Demand for complementary color, like the demand for order in all composition, is compulsive. It seems to be a rule of vision that the eye, seeing one color, will demand its complement. If it is not there, the mind will generate the color spontaneously. Itten says, "The simultaneously generated complement occurs as a sensation in the eye of the beholder, and is not objectively present. It cannot be photographed" (Itten 1961, 87).

To the uninitiated, the principle of simultaneous contrast comes as close as anything to color magic. It can be simply demonstrated, and many of the Bauhaus artists developed logical illustrations. These drawings can be repeated on the computer and extended in exciting ways. But it was left to Josef Albers to illustrate how the concept permeates all aspects of vision to become the fundamental principle of color harmony. Albers's work on the phenomenon is discussed in Chapter 5.

Any serious study of simultaneous contrast must begin with a look at the phenomenon of *after-image*. Your investigation should start with the red circle shown in Figure 2.29. Stare at it without moving your eyes for about thirty seconds, until your eyes have become accustomed to seeing red. Technically, some of the cones in the retina, the receiving surface at the rear of your eye, will become saturated with red information by this process; for the moment you can receive no more red information. After the thirty seconds are up, move your gaze to the white circle shown in Figure 2.30, focusing on the black X at its center. Soon you should see a circle of the blue-green color known as cyan. It may take several tries to make this work because, as with most color phenomena, the more often they are attempted, the clearer they become.

Now let's analyze what has taken place. When that portion of your eye that was focused on the red circle attempted to see the white dot, it was unable to absorb all the components of the white light that reflected from the paper. You could not see any red light; what you saw instead was all of the residual color, the after-image. It was an

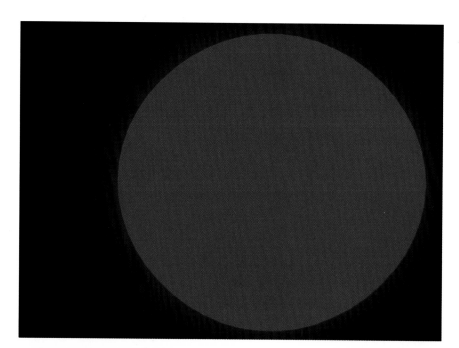

FIGURE 2.29.   After-image.
Computer adaptation from Josef
Albers 1963. (Graphic: the author)

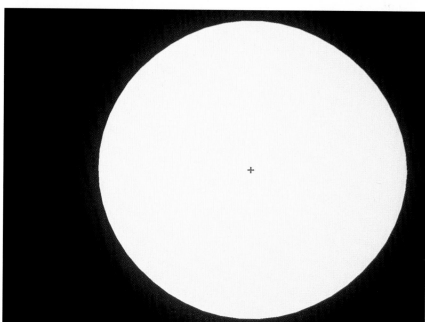

FIGURE 2.30.   After-image.
Computer adaptation from Josef
Albers 1963. (Graphic: the author)

incomplete spectrum of color because it lacked red. The remaining colors, mixed, produced the complement of red—cyan. This phenomenon occurs every time you look at a color. It modifies the perception of each color; it explains why a color will have different appearances with different backgrounds. This simple experiment, fatiguing your eye by looking at a color, is a rudimentary way to find any color's complement.

If you understand the mechanism of simultaneous contrast, you can select colors in anticipation of its effects. Figure 2.31 does this. If you focus on the green and yellow flag for thirty seconds, you can then find the Cuban flag, in its full and correct colors, superimposed on the white rectangle. Computer colors seem to intensify the effect of after-

FIGURE 2.31.   Cuban flag.
(Graphic: Gustus Fischer)

image, providing a way to superimpose all kinds of patterns and forms on the retina of the eye.

This very real phenomenon becomes more than a toy when it is applied to painting, for simultaneous contrast can cause us to see what is sometimes not there; or conversely, to not see what is very carefully placed before us. As Albers has demonstrated (Chapter 5), its effects control virtually every visual experience. Simultaneous contrast can be a powerful design tool; if you understand the mechanism by which it works, you will find it is possible to add colors to a composition by implication, to give or to remove emphasis from any portion of the field of vision.

Vincent van Gogh makes use of simultaneous contrast in *Café at Evening* (Figure 2.32). The use of color here appears simple, resulting in the image of a well-lit café on a brilliant, starry night. Despite its seeming emptiness, the picture vibrates with activity. There are two bold areas of color, the café with its luminous yellow-orange awning and brilliantly illuminated wall, which encloses a floor of orange, and the night with its dazzling blue sky shining above a row of purple-blue buildings. These colors are not complements; each generates a simultaneous contrast that intensifies the colors of the other. The blue sky almost complements the orange of the floor and awning; a few accents of red come close to complementing the green shutters, but they are too orange. The effect is one of intense luminescence. No café light was ever so brilliant, no evening sky so bright. Each color is intensified as it is modified by its missing complement; your eyes are fatigued by the activity of the colors. There is no rest in the starry night, as each color provides an activating complement. There is a vibrancy—a color tension that comes from the simultaneous generation of a complement. The colors seem to dance with activity as each is intensified by the absence of the other. There is no magic in van Gogh's pigment, only a keen sense of how color phenomena can be utilized to maximum advantage.

The computer provides an excellent place to look for colors that will generate spontaneous complements. Figure 2.33 is adapted from a composition by Josef Albers. If you focus on these circles of color, they come alive as each color searches for its complement.

FIGURE 2.32.   Vincent van Gogh, *Café at Evening.* (Collection: State Museum Kroller-Muller, Otterlo, The Netherlands)

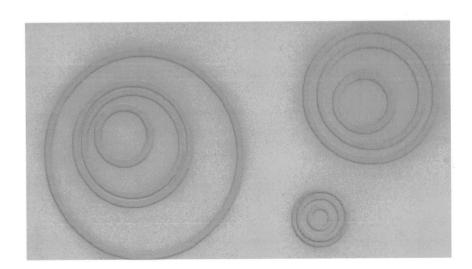

FIGURE 2.33.   Vibrating boundaries. Computer adaptation of a drawing by Josef Albers. (Graphic: William J. Blackmon)

Contrast of Size

There is one more contrast in this long list—the *contrast of size*, or in Itten's words, the "contrast of extension . . . the contrast between much and little, or great and small" (Itten 1973, 104). It is the architect's greatest friend, for it applies as much to the design of space as it does to the selection of color. The façade of the Cathedral of Chartres is often cited for the contrast of its two towers, one big and transparent, the other smaller and more solid.

No composition can be called balanced without a consideration of the size of its elements. The cube in Figure 2.6 uses value contrast effectively, but the drawing is dependent on the contrasting size of the circular opening in the cube in order to achieve a sense of drama and to give the drawing focus. One could develop a general rule calling for a small amount of strong color to balance a larger quantity of weak color, defining "strong" and "weak" as contrast of value, hue, or saturation. This seems to work if balance is the objective; alternatively, contrasts of size can provide a method to achieve dramatic imbalance when that is desired.

Consider the composition in Figure 2.34. A blue-gray color is used sparingly in the drawing and given emphasis by using a small area of each sample. Because of the intense orange ground, the color of the blue is intensified. This is the effect of simultaneous contrast, working with the contrast of size. By eliminating the size difference, as in Figure 2.35, this color reinforcement ceases to exist and the same blue-gray appears as a grayer color.

Coupled with simultaneous contrast, contrast of size can intensify a color, or even introduce motion and space into a composition. Larry Poons, in his painting *Han-San Cadence* (Figure 2.36), has used the effects of simultaneous contrast in a kinetic composition of colors to suggest both movement and depth. The field of small ellipses seems to move in and out of the canvas as the eye finds first a complement and then a noncomplementary color.

FIGURE 2.34.   Contrast of extension. Computer adaptation of a drawing by Johannes Itten. (Graphic: the author)

FIGURE 2.35.   Contrast of extension, modified. (Graphic: the author)

FIGURE 2.36.   Larry Poons, *Han-San Cadence*. 1963. (Courtesy of the Des Moines Art Center, Coffin Fine Arts Trust Fund)

DESIGN APPLICATIONS

It could be concluded that none of Itten's contrasts stand alone. In virtually every example there are elements of more than one contrast; they are interrelated. In color as in art, there is a focus, a theme, a reason for being in every composition. These seven contrasts can show that theme and become an introduction to design with electronic color. To attempt an isolated example of each contrast is a task that can be achieved quickly with the computer. Figures 2.18, 2.19, and 2.20 do this, though the drawings must be regarded as exercises that are not intended to stand alone. As a successful colorist, you will understand which contrasts are involved in any design, and you will know that by orchestrating them to advantage you can occasionally feature the flutes, and sometimes the violins, as each contrast is called upon when appropriate to do what it does best.

With the development of color graphic computers, the color tool Johannes Itten needed now exists. The seven contrasts he defined can be applied in the design of computer graphics, enhancing the usefulness of the computer to both art and architecture. The theories of Itten can now be tested with a persistence that was not feasible before the availability of electronic color. With the computer we can separate the delineation of form from its coloration, providing an opportunity to explore these contrasts through isolation of the color element. Whether in an architectural presentation or a painting, color can be endlessly modified.

It is now possible, in any composition, to study with ease the formal choices the selection of color presents. Perhaps one contrast will be more appealing, or more appropriate to the designer's purpose. These studies are only a step to understanding the color potential of a design. The contrasts of Johannes Itten offer a clear explanation of how objects are seen; they illustrate how the visualization of those objects may be manipulated. The search for form through color was further explored by Josef Albers at the Bauhaus, and is the topic of Chapter 6.

EXERCISES

1. Using just the gray scale of your computer, compose some music; write a song that can be played with just seven notes of color.
2. Do a drawing on the computer screen that divides your screen into a figure-ground pattern of colors. Use only polygons that can be filled with color, for this should not be a line drawing. Next, using these color areas, manipulate the color statement made by your composition to illustrate each of the seven contrasts.
3. Again using variations of a composition, explore the effectiveness of each contrast in achieving depth of composition.

REFERENCES

Itten, Johannes. 1973 [1961]. *The Art of Color: The Subjective Experience and Objective Rationale of Color.* Trans. Ernst van Haagen. New York: Van Nostrand Reinhold.

Whitford, Frank. 1984. *Bauhaus.* London: Thames and Hudson.

Chapter 3

Color Models

E ven the most poetic designer is not disturbed when libraries put numbers on books. People use a card catalog or a computerized index with little trouble, accepting the system as a convenient way to find a book. A library without such a catalog is unthinkable—a collection of thousands or sometimes millions of books without an organizing numerical system in which to file them is beyond comprehension. Why then, when we talk of colors, do we not accept the establishment of a uniform system of filing?

THE NEED FOR ORDER

There are as many colors to be seen as there are books in a library, perhaps more. The manufacturers of computer systems talk of having millions of colors available on their monitors, an array that can be divided into increments finer than the human eye can discern. But there is seldom a system that provides easy access to this collection. Many of us keep using descriptions such as apple green or heavenly blue. The naming of colors is encouraged by the paint and dye industries. Manufacturers of these products establish their own vocabulary, often changing names seasonally or to reflect current fashion. When it comes to selecting or discussing color, we impose on ourselves a totally random system, a library, if you will, without any numbers on the books.

The process of learning a color vocabulary starts in preschool or kindergarten with a box of crayons—we make a mark with the crimson crayon, see the color, and hear the name pronounced; we are beginning to build a color vocabulary in our mind. As we grow older and are promoted to art classes, we are exposed to a different vocabulary on tubes of paint: ultramarine blue, umber, cadmium red. Soon we are graduated and painting our first office or apartment. Now we discover yet another vocabulary: dusty rose, teal, whatever is current. Whether you are an artist, an architect, a designer who makes professional color selections, or an individual concerned with coordinating a personal wardrobe and decorating a room, you are forced into a world of inconsistency. The logical system that you expect when you search for books in the public library is difficult to find when you make color selections.

There was a time, in a far less complicated world, when we could manage with a simpler vocabulary of color. The color choices for painting a house in colonial times were very limited; an enthusiastic pioneer could at best pick from two or three colors that a painter knew how to mix. Color vocabulary was no problem, and like the dozen books he had on his shelf, his paints needed no system of classification.

But the designer's world is different now and changing at a very rapid pace. The eighteenth-century house was totally crafted by hand, on its owner's land; the modern house is assembled from a series of components that can come from all over the world. These pieces are increasingly designed, drawn, and specified by computer. A designer who wants to control and direct the design of an environment today must reckon with the computerized design and selection of materials. That selection increasingly demands a definition of the color of a product as a part of the design package.

The colors that form today's environment are to a large extent determined remotely, in a place far removed from their eventual location, and are often selected by a person unfamiliar with their intended use. Color is applied to building products as they are manufactured. These products are then shipped great distances to be assembled at a construction site or within a space in a building. It is common practice for architects, interior designers, or product designers to do a color board, to arrange all the selected colors for a design in one place, on a board, for presentation to clients. Whereas the choice of materials for a project has been developed methodically, along with the drawings that indicate assembly, the consideration of color is often an afterthought. Only after the design is complete are the manufacturers' samples collected so that colors can be chosen and coordinated. In today's design office, the color board done after the design of a project removes the selection of color from the process of design development and material specification.

Separation of color selection from the design process is not desirable and should not be necessary. Computers can display any color that the eye can see. Further, they are capable of placing an array of colors side by side, locating colors so that the designer's intent is carefully simulated on the computer screen. The selection of color could become a part of the conceptual process. If a project is both drawn and specified by computer, then the selection of colors can become a part of that process; colors could become part of the product specifications that describe the design.

The technology for selecting color by computer is in place today, or could be at any computer workstation used for designing the constructed environment. What is not in place is a uniform system for identifying the different colors. Many systems of color classification exist; most people have heard of one or another method and may in fact have a preferred system. But there is no agreement among these systems. No method of color classification that meets the needs of all those who work with color has been uniformly adopted.

It would seem, then, that we need to devise a universal system for the classification of color. Individuals have risen to the challenge, and proposals do exist. If each approach were not flawed, then one method would find acceptance among all groups and begin to dominate current practice. But the architect sees color with a particular attitude in making the selections for a building; architects demand a neat, straightforward system with a sense of order. It is important to have a system where a visualized color can be found easily, or a sample of color matched. This is a different problem from that which faces a painter mixing paint, for most painters would want a system to explain or to predict what will happen when two pigments were mixed. In the textile business, it is necessary to maintain consistency between dye lots in the manufacturing process; suit coats need to match trousers, blue jeans must be the right color to be recognized as this year's shade of blue. The paint chemist whose job it is to ensure that each can of "chalk white" or "peach pink" is exactly the same has a similar problem. For the manufacturer of color film, or the film processor, color issues are different, more related to color as light. The manufacturer of light bulbs is strictly concerned with the color of light produced by these products. It seems that every profession is doing something slightly different with color information, and has therefore developed slightly different criteria for its classification.

There has been considerable progress in understanding the science of color in the last few years. We are on the threshold of understanding what color is, of knowing how the eye works and how it perceives what is seen. Yet an accepted system for classifying what we see seems as evasive as ever. This dilemma should pose no problem for the computer generation, for techniques are being developed to make computers "translate" one system of information into another. Computers with different operating systems now speak through a translator. However tedious color translations may have been in the past, the problem can be solved. Given the need, a program could be written to translate color information from one system to another. In fact, computers that have such abilities built into their operating hardware are beginning to appear. For the computer specialist, it is a familiar puzzle, the same language problem faced in making one brand of computer "talk" to another.

The problems in finding the perfect color model, the universal system for color classification, are as diverse as the uses for color information. The following survey of color systems will explore some of the more useful proposals for color systems. This is far from an exhaustive list, for the human mind has seen fit to test virtually every conceivable shape in search of a satisfactory color model. Often, what appears to be a solution is but another set of questions.

There is no easy resolution to the geometry of color; piece by piece, we are arriving at a logical understanding of color behavior. It is perhaps a task for the computer finally to reconcile all the demands that would be placed on a perfect color model by the multitude of individuals and professions that could make good use of a logical arrangement of color; or to develop the translator that lets us pass from system to system according to need.

TRADITIONAL CONCEPTS OF COLOR ORGANIZATION

Aristotle believed the eye emitted rays that reached out and brought back color to the viewer. This was obvious, he reasoned, for when the eye was closed, the rays were stopped. This ancient Greek understanding of color was the beginning of a search that has not yet ended, the search for a comprehension of exactly what color is and how the eye functions to receive color information. Aristotelian attitudes dominated Western civilization in the Middle Ages and were not seriously challenged until the Renaissance. Color was not a subject to be questioned, for it had been identified, as was God himself, with light—an element that came directly from the heavens. It was from this beginning that our current systems for color organization evolved.

Aguilonius (1613)

The color imagery of Aguilonius reflects medieval ideas on color in an amusing, yet poetic way. It is typical of the scientific attitudes that began to emerge at the onset of the Renaissance, which were still rooted in the Greek notion of light as the source of color (Gerritsen 1988, 22). In the mind of Aguilonius, the entire spectrum of color was visualized as one beautiful continuity from *albus*, the white of day, to *niger*, the black of night. This spectrum is based on his observation of heavenly phenomena, of the heavens during the course of a day (Figure 3.1). *Rubeus*, the red of the rising and setting sun, assumes the central position halfway between day and night. Anyone who doubts this logic has not stood and watched a sunset, nor observed as the heavens are changed from the white light of day to the black of night. At the midpoint of this transition, the sky is filled with redness. In the diagram *flavus*, or yellow (the source of light) is placed next to white, while blue, *caeruleus*, is close to night and the setting sun. Curiously, this arrrangement parallels the teachings of Kandinsky at the Bauhaus in the early twentieth century (Poling 1986, 58). According to Aguilonius, *rubeus* and the colors of the heavens dominate over *viridis*, the green of the fields, again an observation from nature; the heavens are well separated from the earthly colors in his diagram (Gerritsen 1975, 19).

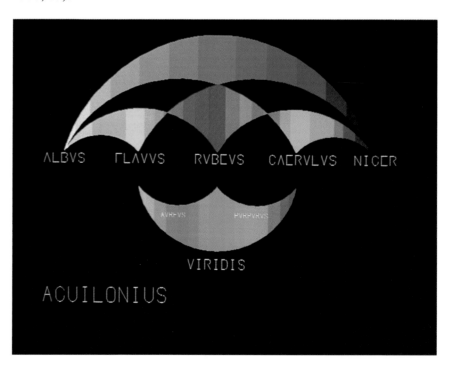

FIGURE 3.1.   Color organization according to Aguilonius, adapted from a sketch by Frans Gerritsen. (Graphic: the author)

Aguilonius took several steps toward the definition of a color system, for there can be found in his proposal a beginning of scientific color observation—an effort to establish a logical base of observed fact. It is a linear system of color organization, a recognition of the continuity of color change from one hue to another. We could begin to establish a "library" of colors, based on the proposals of Aguilonius, though many questions remain unanswered.

Sir Isaac Newton (1660)

The concept of a color wheel—the suggestion that all hues can be arranged around the continuous perimeter of a circle in some sort of logical order—can be attributed to Sir Isaac Newton. He acknowledged that color was a component of light, and saw that in a prism, even such a simple prism as a soap bubble, white light could be broken down into a rainbow of colored lights. Being a man of curiosity, he was intrigued by this fact. He projected light through prisms, creating a band of colors on the walls of his room (Figure 3.2). Observing the order of the hues in this band of color, he saw a progression from red to yellow to green to blue to violet. It was a logical color order, similar to the colors of a rainbow, and it provided a scientific base for color study because it was an observed natural phenomenon (Verity 1980, 34).

Newton took his observations one step further. He noted a similarity between the two ends of the spectrum and experimented with mixing the colors as paint. In this way he achieved purple, the ancient color of royalty and the only hue not found in the rainbow. It was a significant color, a missing link if you will, which could be used as a color connector. He arranged the colors in a circle so that they formed a circular spectrum by connecting both ends, tying violet to red (Figure 3.3); the color wheel was born.

Several ramifications should be noted here in this rather capricious decision on the part of Newton. The connection between red and violet was not based on observation, nor did it have any basis in observable fact. The color circle was a figment of his imagination,

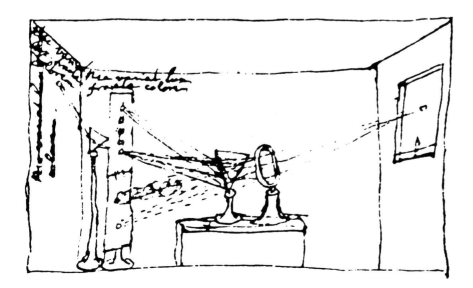

FIGURE 3.2.   Freehand sketch by Newton of one of his experiments on color and light. (Verity 1980, 35)

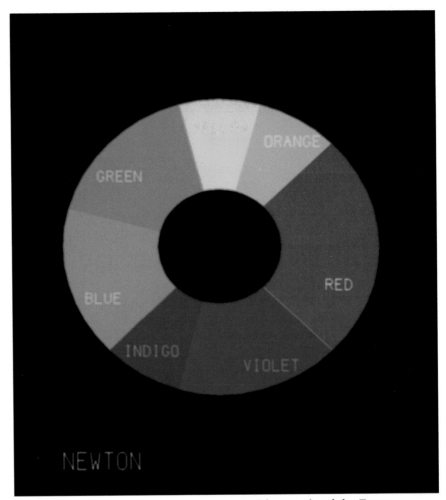

FIGURE 3.3.   Newton's color circle, adapted from a sketch by Frans Gerritsen. (Graphic: the author)

rather than a scientific discovery—a hypothesis, if you will, that has found universal acceptance. It was a keen observation, one with which generations of artists have felt comfortable. Visually, purple does bridge the gap between red and violet in a very convincing fashion, and the principle has become an underlying assumption for virtually every color model since the time of Newton.

Today we understand light as being composed of energy, a "vibration in the form of an extremely large number of elementary units of energy known as quanta" (Verity 1980, 37). The length of this oscillation is measured in nanometers (1 nm = 10^{-9} meters). Some of this energy forms visible light and is called the *visible spectrum*; it is but a small part of the electromagnetic scale (Table 3.1). Visible light occupies the portion of the scale ranging from 380 nm to 750 nm. Red light has a wavelength of 380 nm, violet light of 750 nm. Between these two colors is a linear spectrum of color—orange, yellow, green, blue; the colors of the rainbow arranged exactly as Newton had seen them and noted them. Wavelengths greater than red, beyond 750 nm, are infrared rays, a form of energy not visible to the human eye; wavelengths shorter than violet, less than 380 nm, are the ultraviolet rays,

Table 3.1. The Electromagnetic Scale

Electromagnetic Radiations	Wavelength (millimicron)		
Gamma rays	from	10^{-5} to	10^{-1}
X-rays	from	10^{-3} to	10
Ultraviolet rays	from	10 to	400
Visible rays (light)	from	400 to	700
Infrared rays	from	700 to	10^{5}
Hertzian waves	from	10^{5} to	10^{10}
Radio waves	from	10^{10} to	10^{14}

Source: Adapted from *Verity* 1980, 38.

which are also invisible. The linear nature of this spectrum of color is well established, yet in both the science and the art of color, the circular arrangement of hues proposed by Newton is accepted as a logical and useful color model. Its proposal was an act of genius that transcended the observation of nature and anticipated the modern understanding of color behavior.

There is a difference in coloration between a sunrise and a sunset. The first rays of morning light are tinged with the coolness of ultraviolet as the world emerges from darkness into the light of day. In the evening there is a red glow of sunset as the world is first bathed in the warmth of the sun and then plunged into darkness. Technically the difference can be explained by the properties of the receding or advancing sun. It is like in the spectrum—the dawn coming out of ultraviolet light, forming the daylight and then disappearing into infrared light, and blackness. It demonstrates the linear and repetitive quality of the spectrum.

When systems of color organization such as that proposed by Aguilonius are conceived rather than observed, they can be drawn with perfect proportions and spacing. The colors in Newton's wheel are not equally spaced because they represent a measured observation of physical phenomena. Newton understood that colors are not all of equal weight, that some colors for whatever reason are stronger than others (Gerritsen 1988, 25). This, we have come to realize, is true of color, an expression of the different saturation levels colors achieve. It is another of the elusive problems inherent in the development of a logical color diagram.

Johann Wolfgang von Goethe (1810)

Goethe was one of the first individuals to challenge the logic of Newton's color circle. Rupprecht Matthaei, in his preface to *Goethe's Color Theory*, states:

> It is particularly important to recognize that Newton and Goethe followed totally different aims in their research. While Newton attempted to analyze the nature of light, Goethe applied himself to the phenomenon of color. He wanted "to marvel at color's occurrences and meanings, to admire and, if possible, to uncover color's secrets." (Matthaei 1971, 6)

Goethe proposed a harmonic color circle that addressed the powerful emotions color can evoke. In restructuring the circle, Goethe emphasized six colors, whose origin was more psychological than physical (Matthaei 1971, 44). These colors submit to investigation more easily as a triangle than as a circle, resulting in the harmonic triangle shown in Figure 7.1.

The emotional side of Goethe's triangle, the psychological implications in color decision making, are discussed in Chapter 7. What is to be noted about Goethe's triangle is the complete restructuring along idealistic lines of the color observations made by Newton. What began in the continuous circumference of a circle has been re-formed into a triangle that focuses on three colors: red, yellow, and blue. These hues were identified by Goethe as the fundamental building blocks of color (Matthaei 1971, 191). They can be expressed as the corners of an equilateral triangle. His geometry allowed them to mix —to form secondary shades of orange, green, and purple. The secondary colors could be further combined to form tertiary hues. The identification of three primary colors was done partly on an emotional basis, partly on physical grounds. It was an idea later pursued with vigor by the Bauhaus artists.

Sir James Clerk Maxwell (1872)

By the end of the nineteenth century, the color wheel was accepted as a logical color ordering. The circular color order had been examined by many individuals; numerous descriptions and spacings had been proposed that, for one reason or another, represented logical points of view. The two hundred odd years between the Renaissance and the beginning of modern times had seen the search for a logical color model pass many times from physicist to painter and from psychologist to physiologist, with each contributing to an understanding of color behavior (Verity 1980, 125).

James Maxwell, a Scottish physicist, brought mathematical order to the search for a color model. Maxwell was involved in research on the electromagnetic wave spectrum, which he submitted to a careful mathematical analysis. From his studies of the electromagnetic theory of light, he developed in 1872 a chart in the form of an equilateral triangle (Figure 3.4). He suggested that all known colors could be located within this triangle. The triangle is clearly indebted to Goethe, for the similarities are many: Each is an equilateral triangle; each identifies three colors as primaries; and each combines the colors to include other hues in the center of the triangle. Here, however, the similarities stop (Verity 1980, 49).

The Maxwell triangle identifies red, green, and blue as the three primary components of light, the primary colors at the corners of the triangle. These are the same colors that today are the basis of both television and computer color monitors. They are the primary colors of light, rather than of pigment. In the center of the chart is located white—the color produced by the combination of all components of the spectrum. All colors can now be arranged within the triangle. As one moves along its edges, the transitions observed by Newton are experienced: Red changes to orange, then to yellow, and finally to green; green changes to blue; blue changes to violet, to purple, and back to red. Moving from the edge to the center of the triangle, the brilliance of each primary color is lost in a transition from full saturation at the edge to white at the center.

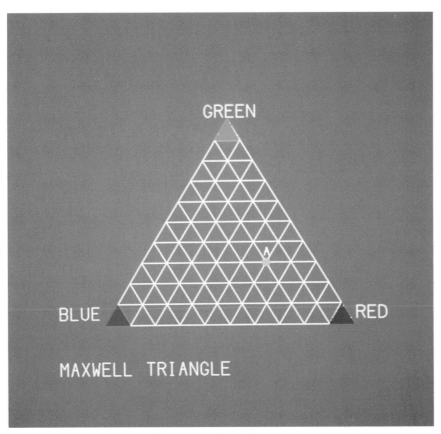

FIGURE 3.4.   The Maxwell triangle. (Graphic: the author)

Over the triangle of continuously changing colors Maxwell super-imposed a grid, lines drawn parallel to each edge of the triangle, in order to establish a system of color notation. Any point within the triangle identifies a specific color sample, and was assumed by Max-well to be definable by the quantities of the primary color it contains. This quantity can be measured, he postulated, by the distance from each primary color. In Figure 3.4, the tiny orange point noted as A is located five steps from red, seven steps from green, and eight steps from blue. The unique color that point A represents is given a numer-ical address: 5R/7G/8B. A simple numbering system could, in theory, identify any color that exists and provide a method for quantifying the science of color.

The equilateral triangle, as Euclid discovered, has many unique qualities of its own. In Maxwell's triangle any point—any color—could be defined by only two dimensions, the distance from point 1 and point 2. Thus orange could be defined, excluding the properties of its lightness, by percentages of red and green, by percentages of red and blue, or in fact by percentages of blue and green. Point A in Figure 3.4 can be described as five steps from red or seven steps from green; or equally well as five steps from red and eight steps from blue.

It would be simpler to define a color with only two coordinates, and still simpler if those coordinates were rectilinear. This is possible, for it is one of the properties of an equilateral triangle that when its area is transformed to an equivalent right-angle triangle, the geomet-

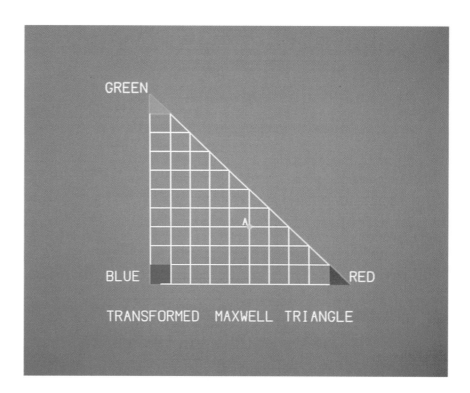

FIGURE 3.5. The modified Maxwell triangle. (Graphic: the author)

ric properties of each part remain constant. This permits the modification of Maxwell's equilateral triangle into a right-angled triangle without changing the relationship of its parts to the whole. The resulting coordinate grid of lines has become rectilinear. In Figure 3.5, the triangle has been modified. Point A is still orange, the same point identified in the original triangle. It is still five steps from red and seven steps from green. 5R/7G is a formula that will locate that point. Any point can be located in this way with total consistency.

Maxwell's discoveries were a revelation for the science of color. Unfortunately, the painters of the world, those who work with pigments and who look upon these systems as a clue to the mixing of color, were left behind. While the abstraction of transforming the triangle from equilateral to right-angled did marvelous things for the science of color, it removed the color model from being visually descriptive of color behavior. A painter, or an architect selecting colors, can relate to Newton's wheel; but by the time these colors have been modified into the right-angled triangle, the visual relationship to color behavior has been lost. Red and green have been identified as primary, blue as secondary, without any visual logic, in order to produce a mathematical simplification. It is extremely difficult to find one model that will meet the needs of all.

Albert H. Munsell (1915)

Any system for modeling color that is fully to categorize all of the colors must recognize three fundamental qualities of color: hue, lightness, and saturation. Variations in these terms develop between different color models; for a description of each of these qualities, see the discussion on the theory of contrasts in Chapter 2.

Remember that there are three qualities of color and not two, for the result is a three-dimensional color model rather than a chart. Several such models were developed in the nineteenth century, including those of Runge, Wundt, Von Bezold, and others (Gerritsen 1975, 22). If the colors are to be arrayed along coordinates as Maxwell proposed, then they will form a three-dimensional graph, not a chart. When you discuss light this is not as important, for the third quality, lightness, becomes a matter of quantity. When you mix pigment, however, this is not true.

Although Albert Munsell was not the first person to propose a three-dimensional color model, in 1915 he developed a system that has enjoyed enormous popularity. This model has been extensively published and has been favored by architects, painters, and even paint manufacturers. For architects it is probably the most accepted system of color notation yet devised (Figure 3.6). Munsell was an American art teacher who approached the modeling of color with the eyes of a painter rather than a physicist. His color notation is a three-dimensional system for classifying pigment and not light.

Hue was defined by Munsell as the familiar circle of hues, though their spacing has been reproportioned. Munsell chose to designate five primary colors: red (R), yellow (Y), green (G), blue (B), and purple (P). These five colors, together with their complements: yellow-red (YR), green-yellow (GY), blue-green (BG), purple-blue (PB), and red-purple (RP), provide a ten-part division that suggests a decimal system (Figure 3.7). The hues, samples of which are published in a book of standard colors (Munsell 1976), are spaced equally around the hue circuit. By colorometric measurement they represent consistent steps of hue change, equal gradations to which anyone trained in the visual arts can relate. As a result of reproportioning the hue circuit, Munsell caused changes in the definition of complementary colors, which to

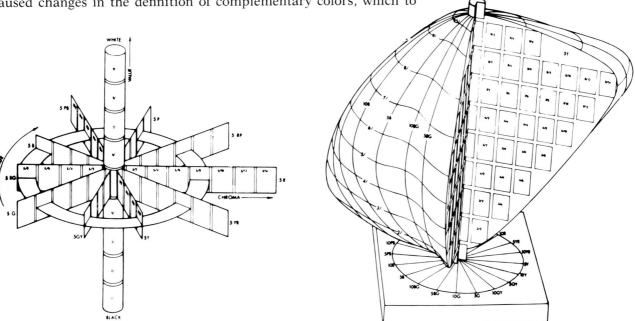

FIGURE 3.6.   Munsell color solid with one quarter removed to show constant hue 5Y. (The Munsell name and Munsell Color Space are trademarks of Kollmorgen Corp. Permission to use granted by Munsell Color, Baltimore, MD.)

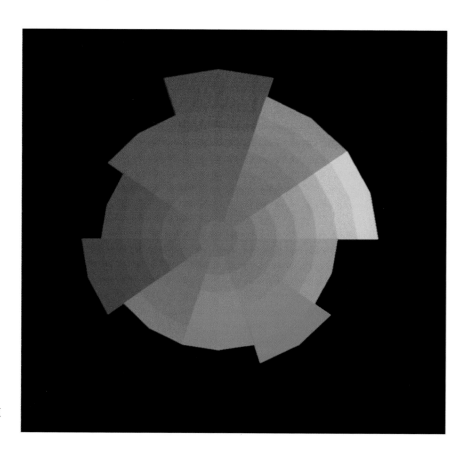

FIGURE 3.7.   A circle of Munsell hues. (Graphic: Clifford D. Kinard III and Timothy D. Williams)

some people is disturbing. True complements are either not as they have been shown experimentally to be, or else they are not in opposing positions on the Munsell model.

Value—as Munsell called the second color dimension—is similar to lightness, though related more to pigment that to light. Black and white form the vertical axis of the color model. This axis extends from white, absolutely pure white (the presence of all color) on the top, to ideal black (the absence of all color) on the bottom. Although neither of these ideal poles is attainable in pigment, the steps between them are highly definable as grays. They are numbered from 1 to 10 on a decimal scale. The grays, like the hues, are equally spaced visually and published in *The Munsell Book of Color* (Munsell 1976).

Chroma—Munsell's term for the third dimension of color—is similar to saturation, though to Munsell it relates more to the amount of colorant present in the pigment. It is in this definition of chroma that Munsell's color model differs substantially from all previous proposals. While the circle of hues includes all conceivable hues, and while the value axis is all-inclusive, Munsell realized that new colorants were constantly being devised. Chroma is therefore an open-ended commodity that radiates outward from the central axis of the model. It is a convenient arrangement, for as new and more intense colorants are discovered, they can be added to the end of the line, extending the available chromas for any given hue without having to redefine each color to accommodate it. This gives the Munsell color model its characteristic random appearance. If a perfect geometric system were used as a color standard—a sphere, for example—color samples would have to be adjusted each time a brighter chroma was devised.

During the last fifty years there has been considerable expansion of the Munsell model as brighter colors and colorants have been discovered. The phosphors used in computer systems have expanded the Munsell colors by some 40 percent. Frederick Simon, investigating Munsell color samples on the computer, states:

> The matte edition of the Munsell Book of Color contains 1030 samples. . . . However, the VDU (video display unit) simulation has 1670 "samples" for comparable limits; the gain is naturally in the regions of high chroma made possible by the phosphors used in video monitors. (Simon 1986, 6)

The *Munsell Book of Color* is organized in a series of vertical sections, or cuts, through the color model. Each page contains a particular hue, and displays the array of values and chromas that exist for that hue (Figures 3.8, 3.9, and 3.10). If more saturated chromas are developed, they can be added to the samples. The point of maximum chroma for each page of this chart is at a different level, depending upon its value. This open-ended book currently contains approximately 1,150 discrete color samples (Munsell 1976).

Many of our intuitions about color are explained using the Munsell system. Variations in lightness, always present in color considerations, occur as vertical points through the model. Color mixture is linear between any two points. Most important, all colors that occur at any given value level have a constant value or lightness; therefore, in the development of computer graphics, hue changes in a drawing can be explored without causing undesirable shifts in the contrast of value. When you work with the computer, it is essential to have carefully memorized a model such as the Munsell model, in order to find the colors that you will need.

The CIE Chromaticity Chart (1931)

In 1931 the Commission Internationale de l'Eclairage assembled in Cambridge, England, to establish a world standard for the measurement of color (Gerritsen 1975, 65). By that time modern instrumentation had made it possible to measure with fair accuracy the wavelength of any particular colored light. The commission took as its model the principles established sixty years earlier by James Maxwell; it selected three standard colors, a particular red, a green, and a blue, with which to generate a version of the Maxwell triangle. The result was what is known as the CIE chromaticity chart, which became a standard in the lighting industry for measuring the color of light. Figure 3.11 shows a computer drawing of the chart, though it must be considered a simulation; the many colors involved in rendering each hue and saturation are beyond the capacity of the computer used. In 1976 the CIE chart was revised to create a more even distribution of colors. The revised chart, now indicating colors in "uniform color space," is the current standard for measuring the color of light (Figure 3.12).

It is easy to discern the Maxwell triangle in this chart. Standard blue is located in the lower-left-hand corner, standard green in the upper-left-hand corner, and standard red in the lower-right corner; in each case, the corners represent 100 percent of the light of a particular

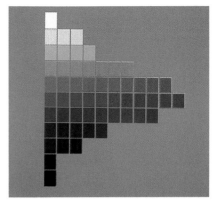

FIGURE 3.8.   Munsell value/ chroma chart—red. (Graphic: Clifford D. Kinard III and Timothy D. Williams)

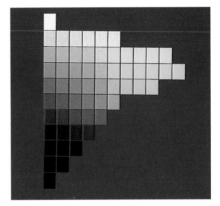

FIGURE 3.9.   Munsell value/ chroma chart—yellow. (Graphic: Clifford D. Kinard III and Timothy D. Williams)

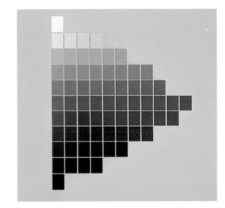

FIGURE 3.10.   Munsell value/ chroma chart—blue. (Graphic: Clifford D. Kinard III and Timothy D. Williams)

wavelength and 0 percent of any other color. The diagram never defines white; rather, it illustrates the ambiguity of white as a concept. Somewhere in the center of the diagram is the "white spot," that point where light from the three sources blends to form white light. Sunlight is one spot on the diagram and incandescent light another. That this point is not fixed, as it is in the Munsell model, is useful in describing the color of light from various light sources without implying a deviation from some established norm. The absolute white at the top of a Munsell model is, after all, theoretical. Itten has suggested that cold–warm contrast is always relative and is not determined from any absolute point (see Chapter 2).

The triangle that forms the border of this chart is not filled with color, as in the Maxwell triangle. The "perfect" red, blue, and green defined by international accord are no more attainable than is the ideal, absolute white at the top of the Munsell color model. The characteristic curve around the colored area in the diagram represents a plot of fully saturated hues, the color circle proposed by Newton.

A tour of these hues reveals several points of interest to the colorist. Beginning at blue, at the low end of the visible spectrum, the eye climbs quickly into the green area—the chart is in fact dominated by the influence of green. Green, measured at about 520 nm, is the center of the visible spectrum, and predictably it is the easiest light source to attain. Among the hues, it is capable of the greatest brilliance. As the eye moves toward the high end of the spectrum at the reds, it is

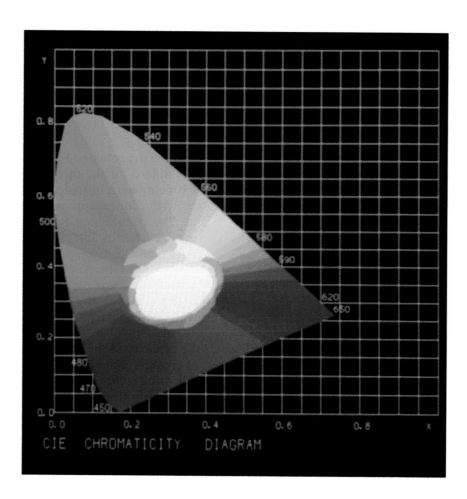

FIGURE 3.11. Computer simulation of the CIE chromaticity chart. (Graphic: the author)

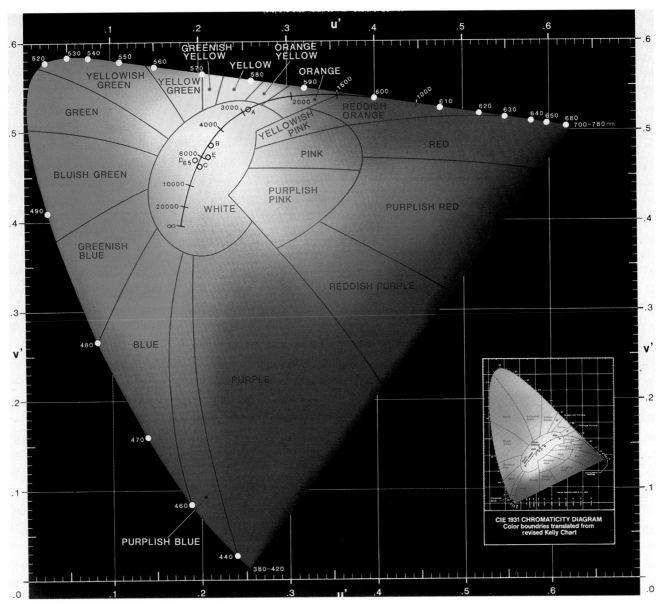

FIGURE 3.12.   CIE 1976 UCS chromaticity diagram, also showing (inset)
the CIE 1931 chromaticity diagram. (Permission granted by Photo Research
Division of Kollmorgen Instruments Corporation to reproduce CIE diagrams)

difficult to attain a highly saturated red; red quickly becomes infrared
heat, without any visible light source. Perhaps most interesting is the
plot of hues between red and blue, showing how they in fact are linear;
this line is the connecting link between red and blue drawn so long
ago by Sir Isaac Newton; it is a plot of those purple colors that do not
exist naturally in the spectrum of light. The perimeter of the chart is
a quantified recalculation of the circle of colors originally proposed
by Newton.

To find the position on the chart of a particular sample of colored
light, a correct percentage of red light and of green light must be
found. The color is then located at an appropriate distance from each
source—red and green. The technical design of a color monitor for a

computer begins with this chart. Three points on the chart are identified, forming a triangle incorporating as large a color area as possible. Phosphors that emit the light defined by these points are then selected as light sources for the picture tube. To design a monitor with a large color capability, we want to select light sources as close to the corners of the chart as possible; within the triangle connecting these points lie all the colors these phosphors are capable of producing. No colors beyond the triangle can be attained unless additional light sources are used.

We could never achieve a correctly colored rendition of the chromaticity chart on a computer. As long as there are only three light sources, a portion of this chart will be beyond its reach. The phosphors selected today emulate light insofar as possible from the corners of this curve.

The development of the chromaticity diagram was a critical step in the search for an ideal color model; it is a method by which the light generated from computer phosphor guns can be measured and quantified. If one were to liken this diagram to the Munsell model, it is a hue-saturation diagram—approximating a horizontal section through the Munsell model. While the positions of the colors in the chart are measurable, many designers do not find them memorable; it is a shape with perhaps more appeal to the physicist for its logic than to the artist for its explanation of color behavior.

Frans Gerritsen (1975)

The effort to find an ideal color model was continued by the work of Frans Gerritsen, who in 1975 developed a color space that is both responsive to computer color generation and indicative of logical color relationships (Gerritsen 1975). The Gerritsen model is based on the familiar black-white pole of the Munsell space. But unlike the Munsell model, it contains six primary colors—the red, green, and blue of the chromaticity diagram and their complements: cyan (blue-green) magenta, and yellow. Unlike the chromaticity chart, Gerritsen's model is three-dimensional (Figure 3.13).

There are many similarities between the Gerritsen and Munsell models. Gerritsen, however, proposes a model that is geometrically perfect. On the Gerritsen model, the perimeter ring of saturated hues rises and falls in a geometric curve reflecting the lightness of the individual hue at its maximum saturation. The model responds to both additive and subtractive color mixing (These terms are discussed in Chapter 1). Six primary colors are identified: the three primary colors of light, red, green, and blue, and their complements: cyan, magenta, and yellow. Figure 3.14 shows the model as seen from the top and indicates how, by spacing colors equally around a circle, it is possible to place complementary colors in opposing positions. The hues are so balanced that a mixture of complements at an adequately small scale on the computer screen will produce a gray color, a color void of any hue suggestion.

Vertical sections cut through the model illustrate the balanced, geometric nature of Gerritsen's concept. Figure 3.15 is a section through the center of the sphere displaying primary blue and yellow. It shows the value-chroma array of each hue. The white–black axis

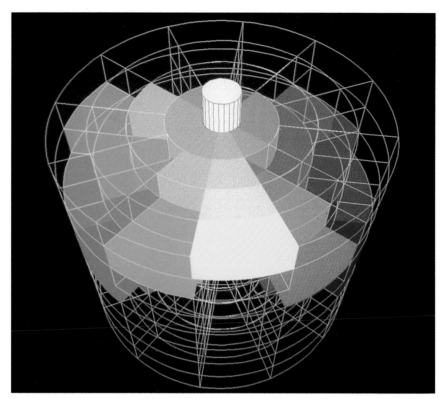

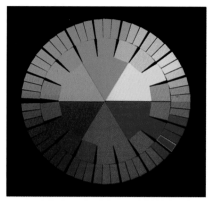

FIGURE 3.14.   The six primary colors of the Gerritsen system and their mixture. (Graphic: Trey Beatty)

FIGURE 3.13.   The Gerritsen color space. (Graphic: Gwinn Gibson Harvey and John M. Young, Jr.)

runs vertically in the center of the illustration. At yellow, the saturated tip of the hue circle rises to its highest point on the circumference. This is in accord with both observation and measurement, for saturated yellow is the lighest of the saturated hues. At blue, the saturated tip falls to its lowest point, balancing perfectly the rise of its complement. This too is in agreement with the nature of the color.

The section illustrated in Figure 3.16 is through green and its complement, magenta. These two colors, when fully saturated, are very close in value to a middle gray. Magenta rises only slightly above the center of the model; green falls a bit below. Note that in each section the colors with a constant value occur on a horizontal line. Neither changes of hue nor of saturation would affect the contrast of value in the design of a graphic composition using this model. Figure 3.17 is the section through red-cyan. In this case the values of the saturated hues, light for cyan and dark for red, are seen at points equidistant from the extremes of the other two sections.

Gerritsen, in his perfect geometric model, has hypothesized a series of color relationships that can be formed in the mind as a simple picture. It is a map of all the colors, to be memorized. Using it, a designer could find a particular color in a simple and logical fashion. Visually it is a model that describes the way in which color behaves. Recall the various Itten contrasts discussed in Chapter 2: contrast of value (values are all horizontally stratified in the model for easy access regardless of the other color characteristics); contrast of hue (each hue is arranged in orderly fashion around the perimeter of the model in visually equal steps); contrast of saturation (saturation is simply de-

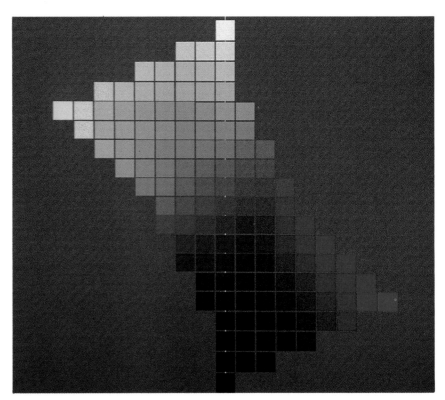

FIGURE 3.15. The Gerritsen color space, section through blue-yellow. (Graphic: the author)

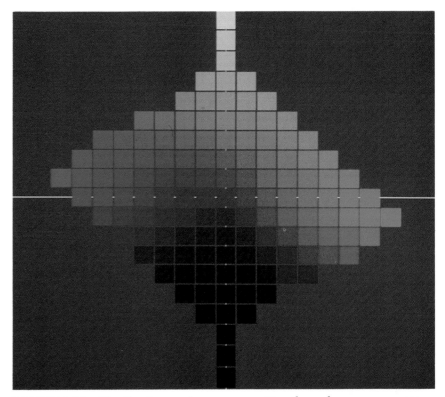

FIGURE 3.16. The Gerritsen color space, section through green- magenta. (Graphic: the author)

FIGURE 3.17.   The Gerritsen color space, section through red-cyan. (Graphic: the author)

fined for each hue along a line from the vertical axis to the perimeter); cold–warm contrast (cooler colors are on one side of the model, warmer ones on the other); complementary contrast (opposing colors in the model are exact complements). This is a model that should find great appeal in the world of art.

The Gerritsen model has not been quantified, as have the CIE diagram and the Munsell space. As a theory of color behavior, it is only a hypothesis. But the model is an object of geometric beauty, a construction that can be committed to memory and recalled in order to make intuitive color selections and decisions. In this way Gerritsen has satisfied many of the designer's needs and provided a tool for understanding color relationships.

COMPUTER COLOR SELECTION

There are many ways to tell a computer what color to use: There is no industry standard, nor is there a system that could be claimed as ideal. The simplest color computers offer a choice of only eight colors, and these are generally selected by number. At the other extreme, complex professional workstations are capable of displaying over 16 million colors on a monitor (Mitchell 1987, 42). Most computers have some built-in color model, perhaps even a choice of systems for the selection of color. Several systems are available, and some terminals even offer a choice of systems. Included here is a survey of the most common methods of color selection provided by today's computer systems.

RGB Specification

The most elementary means of controlling color on a computer monitor is by RGB specification—specifying the percentage of red, of green, and of blue light required for each color. There is an inherent simplicity to this, and from an engineering point of view it is totally logical. It corresponds directly to the internal arrangement of the computer equipment, although, as with so many things in computers, human logic and machine logic are two different commodities. It is extremely difficult to picture most colors, based on a percentage of these three components.

Usually, computers with this arrangement will show a sample on the screen of the color being mixed, so that by trial and error the desired color may be found. This makes selection simpler, but it does not help the individual who wants a darker value of the same color, or a less saturated color. We usually think in terms of value, or hue, or saturation in searching for a color, or perhaps in terms of one of the other color contrasts discussed in Chapter 2, for we are usually building a composition of contrasts. These contrasts are memorable color phenomena that we can anticipate intuitively. Red-green-blue transitions are not easily remembered, since they are not visual phenomena within the artist's usual experience.

If we take the three source colors, red, green, and blue, as variables, it is possible to construct a color model using the colors as parameters in the same way that three-dimensional models are built with hue, value, and saturation. Such a model is shown in Figure 3.18. The edges of the form can easily be imagined—the gradual transition from blue to red, for example, is not hard to picture. But as soon as a third color is introduced into the mixture, selecting a color from that

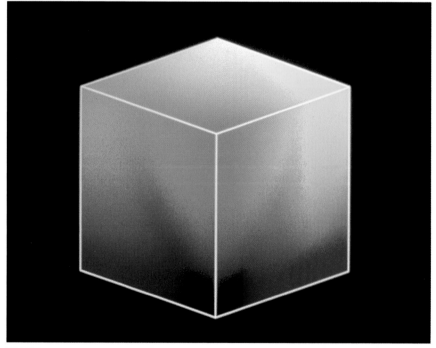

FIGURE 3.18.   Tektronix RGB color space. (Courtesy of Tektronix, Inc.)

vast quantity of color within the model, all visual relationship to color experience is lost.

Painters have dealt with this problem for years. They mix two colors, or three colors, on a palette and learn to predict the resulting color. But red, green, and blue presents a very limited palette of colors, requiring careful adjustment to achieve a full and diverse range of color. A good computer is capable of this fine adjustment, is able to achieve the limitless variety of color that is needed, but for most individuals this degree of subtlety requires great patience and much experience. More often than not, the search becomes a continual trial and error process.

CIE Uniform Color Space

The CIE chromaticity diagram discussed in this chapter has proved to be an excellent tool for measuring light. As a two-dimensional plot of hue and saturation characteristics, it is a logical point for beginning computer color mixture. Values can be added to the chart by gradually reducing the intensity (brightness) of the light source until all light is removed and absolute black is achieved. Thus the chromaticity chart can be extruded into a three-dimensional color model known as the CIE uniform color space (Boll 1986, 8).

The base of this form is the familiar chromaticity chart shown in Figure 3.12. By imagining a neutral gray axis extending from the white point at the center of the chart upward toward absolute black, and by arraying each color in each layer of the chart horizontally from its corresponding gray point, a three-dimensional color model is achieved.

Most of the color models discussed in this chapter are regularly shaped objects possessing a strong sense of beauty through their geometric order; in this regard, CIE color space is more like an extraneous export from the Rocky Mountains! The curve that forms the perimeter of the chromaticity chart cannot be extended evenly toward the black point at the top of this model—as light sources, red, green, and blue do not lose brightness at an even rate. The fluctuations of form create valleys and ridges on the surface of this mountain of light, giving it a highly irregular form.

To this mountain now comes the designer, light pen or some other graphic device in hand, to make color selections for a design. Any point within the color space is instantly definable, measurable so that its color becomes a known commodity. A manufacturer finds this important because the colors generated on the computer are defined and can be translated to other parts of the manufacturing process. In today's textile plants, pattern colors are selected by computer (Boll 1986, 9). With these colors quantified, the color information can be linked directly to the automated looms that weave textiles. As the textile industry becomes more automated, the colors that appear in clothing and fashion, as well as the textiles that form a critical part of most architectural interiors, could be selected by computer.

The use of CIE color space as a color model has been demonstrated with considerable success. What is gained in accuracy and scientific predictability, however, is lost in its failure to present the designer with a memorable visual imagery for intuitive color selection. For example, defining a desired change in value usually forces changes in all color dimensions, or conversely, requires one to steer an amoebic path through this mountain of color. For the designer, this would seldom be the system of choice.

CIE color space provides a sound technical method for measuring colored light; its technical competence in this area is proved. One only wonders why it must be imposed on the design profession. The translation of any color from CIE color space to another model is a mathematical problem, no doubt an enormously complicated mathematical problem, but then computers are capable of enormously complicated math. The CIE system is a better friend to the physicist than to the designer.

HLS Specification

The selection of colors from a model based on the contrast of hue, lightness, and saturation would appear to provide a color selection method consistent with the needs of most designers. Such systems are increasingly available on computers. An elementary color space, based on hue, lightness, and saturation, is illustrated in Figure 3.19.

But one must be cautious in using these terms. Of the color models explored in this chapter, only those proposed by Albert Munsell and Frans Gerritsen have maintained hues of a constant value at the same level in the color space. In the other models, a change in hue is accompanied by a corresponding adjustment in the value (brightness). This results in a perimeter of rising and falling values around the model; value shifts occur every time the hue is changed—an unnecessary complication, but one that can be worked with if it is understood. This rise and fall of values around the hue circle is apparent in Figure 3.20.

Munsell and Gerritsen also differ in their definition of saturation change. With Munsell, the divisions of saturation (chroma) are arranged in visually constant steps, while on the Gerritsen model they are expressed as percentages of change from zero to total saturation. Figure 3.21 illustrates a section through the green-magenta portion of a typical HLS color model. At the midpoint vertically, a uniform gray value is seen, extended from the neutral core to the fully saturated hues on the left and the right. There is some inconsistency in this value scale, perhaps not enough to matter if one is not being overly critical. But compare this to Figure 3.22, a section through the red-cyan portion of the space, or even more dramatically to Figure 3.23, where the blue-yellow section is shown. Dramatic shifts in value are seen as the eye moves horizontally through the color space. Any change in hue using this model will be accompanied by an unpredictable change in value.

A comparison of the Gerritsen sections and those of an HLS system suggests other differences, for the HLS model has become almost square. With HLS, each horizontal line is a percentage of saturation, a simple way of identifying colors to the computer, but a cause of distortion of the model; each step in the top and bottom rows represents a much smaller change in saturation than is to be found in the critical center row.

For a designer, the HLS color model is an improvement over RGB

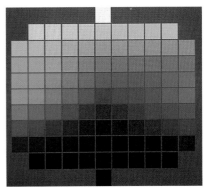

FIGURE 3.21.   HLS color space, section through green-magenta (Graphic: the author)

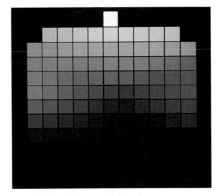

FIGURE 3.22.   HLS color space, section through red-cyan. (Graphic: the author)

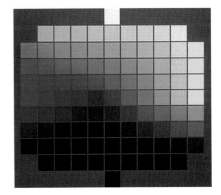

FIGURE 3.23.   HLS color space, section through blue-yellow. (Graphic: the author)

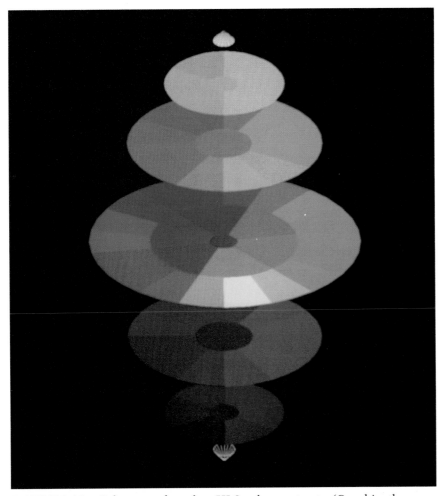

FIGURE 3.19.   Color space based on HLS color contrasts. (Graphic: the author)

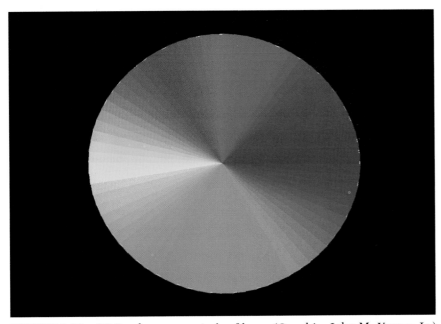

FIGURE 3.20.   HLS color space, circle of hues. (Graphic: John M. Young, Jr.)

color specification. Color is specified in identifiable, memorable terms that permit an intuitive approach to selection; this does not begin to approach the logic of the better theoretical models. However, by appreciating both the weaknesses and strengths of each color space and making appropriate design adjustments, a designer using HLS models will have a tool for creating remarkable color graphics. The graphics in this book have been defined using this system.

The HVC Color Solid

In the patient search for a workable color space, it is clear that a standard of measurement must be found. Where, after all, would architectural form be today if each designer were inventing his or her own meter stick? In many professions, the CIE diagram is adequate and exacting. It has become a standard in the illumination industry. For the graphic designer it is not a logical model, but it can be a unit of measure—the standard against which any model is measured.

The HVC color solid is a proposal by Tektronix, Inc., based on the CIE diagram. The model is based on hue, value, and chroma, all familiar terms to the designer and arranged in a familiar manner (Figure 3.24). The edge of the model is random, as it must be, for constant values are maintained at a uniform level; the maximum chroma of each of the six primary–secondary hues seeks its own value level. Colors can therefore be found intuitively within the color space—values are constant on any horizontal line, saturations are constant on any vertical line. In reference to standard Munsell numbering, a standard red has been assigned to zero on the hue circuit (Taylor 1988).

What is unique about this model is its reference to the CIE 1976 UCS chromaticity diagram and specifically to the 9300K as the white point on that chart (Figure 3.12). The model illustrated in Figure 3.24 is specific to a particular computer monitor and illustrates its peculiar

FIGURE 3.24. The HVC color solid from three perspectives. (Courtesy of Tektronix, Inc.)

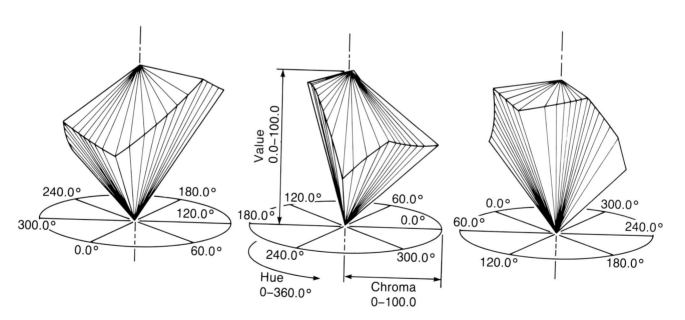
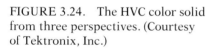

chromatic character. Seen on another computer, this model might look very different, illustrating a different color capability. Yet because of the common reference, a given color would appear the same on each computer. Each would be referenced to CIE space. Using this principle, any computer screen and printing device can be calibrated to the CIE standard. A color seen on one device would appear exactly like that color on another.

This is not an "ultimate" color model, only an expression of one machine's capability. But for the graphic designer it could be a convenient working tool, because it is based on a uniform display of color space. As long as the model is calibrated to the CIE standard, different computers and display devices become interchangeable; colors become consistent across many devices. As a designer, you are free to select colors, and you can communicate your selections by wire around the world.

Paint Systems

Much of the work of graphic designers today is being done on "paint systems" developed by various computer manufacturers. These systems function using most of the methods discussed for selecting color, and they generally include several useful techniques of altering the color for each screen pixel. Often they include one other capability: that of producing a ramp of colors (color ramps are discussed in Chapter 4). From an assortment of colors displayed on the computer screen, two samples are identified. The computer will then produce a gradation of color in any number of steps, making a transition from one color to the other. This is a ramp.

The blending of colors in color ramp can simulate the effects of a watercolor wash or even produce a few visual tricks that would be difficult to achieve in watercolor. Blends are responsible for some of the more interesting effects seen in today's computer graphics. No discussion of computer color selection would be complete without mention of them.

The color ramp is particularly useful in rendering architectural surfaces; in Figure 3.25 the rounded forms of a building are made understandable by a ramp of color as the color of the surface is blended toward white. A more subtle use of the ramp appears in Figure 3.26, where an architectural fragment is illuminated by sunlight. In Figure 3.27, this same fragment is seen as it would appear by moonlight. The surfaces of these illustrations are not flat areas of color, they are composed of strips—adjacent polygons—with each step rendered in a variation of the adjacent color. (Paint systems automatically create color ramps, but the colors in these illustrations have been individually chosen.)

These last illustrations form a careful architectural display of the use of cold–warm contrast. In order to achieve subtlety of color, one must have careful control of hue, value, and saturation—memorable color commodities. The order, the beauty, of a machine-derived progression can fall short of one's expectations without meticulous color control. But sensitively used, color ramps can shape an architectural surface, bringing life to it and animating it with a source of light and of color.

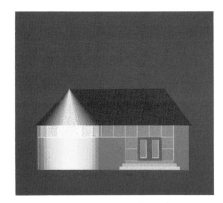

FIGURE 3.25. Study for a house. (Graphic: Amy Kay Stubbs)

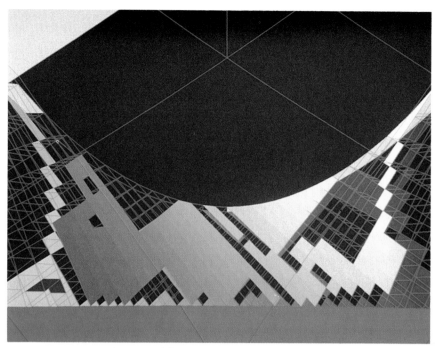

FIGURE 3.26.   Architectural fragment in sunlight. (Graphic: John M. Young, Jr.)

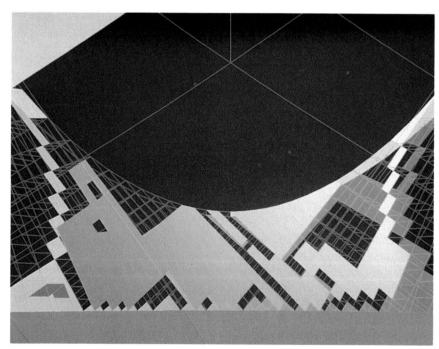

FIGURE 3.27.   Architectural fragment seen by the light of the moon. (Graphic: John M. Young, Jr.)

INVENTING A COLOR SPACE

To speak the language of color, one must have both a color vocabulary and an understanding of how colors interact. This requires a familiarity with some system of order—a color model. There is a need for a reasonable color standard that is both scientifically exacting and adequately pictorial. One system that responds to both needs does not appear to exist. If we could find a perfect system, it would probably have two characteristics: colorametric accuracy and visual simplicity. First, it would be colorametrically accurate. Any color generated on a monitor should have a numerical value that could be shared with a client, patron, or customer. The Commission Internationale d'Eclairage has established standards that should make this possible; the published standards of the Munsell system provide a useful alternative. Second, it should be visually descriptive of color phenomena. Complementary colors should be perceived as complements; lighter hues should be perceived as light, darker hues as dark. The contrasts of hue, lightness, and saturation should be geometrically discernible. Changes in saturation should be possible without altering lightness or hue; each variable should be visual and controllable on a model that could be committed to memory.

But although all these features are desirable, they do not need to be built into the computer you are using. It is possible to formulate your own color model; probably no better way exists for understanding the differences between systems than to draw your own understanding of color relationships. Any system of your own design can be generated on the screen as a way of learning color differences, and committed to memory. It may not be a part of your computer system, but you can still draw with it using available techniques and have it for your own reference. A color model is, after all, only another tool for accessing colors. By drawing models, by working with the structure of color, you can commit to memory a mental image of color relationships. Only with such relationships clearly in mind can you produce good color design.

EXERCISES

1. Explore the color potential of your computer to determine what color models it contains.
2. Examine some of the available color models by drawing them, as a way of familiarizing yourself with their differences.
3. Draw your own color model in order to become familiar with color differences and to explore the means at your disposal for selecting colors.

REFERENCES

Boll, Harold. 1986. The role of a color space in computer aided design. Paper read at Clemson University Computer Color Graphics Conference, 8–9 April, Greenville, SC.

Gerritsen, Frans. 1975. *Theory and Practice of Color*. New York: Van Nostrand Reinhold.

Gerritsen, Frans. 1988. *Evolution in Color*. West Chester, PA: Schiffer Publishing.

Matthaei, Rupprecht, ed. 1971. *Goethe's Color Theory*. American ed. New York: Van Nostrand Reinhold.

Mitchell, William J., Robin S. Liggett, and Thomas Kvan. 1987. *The Art of Computer Graphics Programming*. New York: Van Nostrand Reinhold.

Munsell, Albert. 1976 [1924]. *The Munsell Book of Color*. Baltimore: Munsell Color Company, Inc.

Munsell, Albert. 1969. *A Grammar of Color: A Basic Treatise on the Color System of Albert H. Munsell*. Ed. and with an intro. by Faber Birren. New York: Van Nostrand Rienhold.

Poling, Clark V. 1986. *Kandinsky's Teaching at the Bauhaus: Color Theory and Analytical Drawing*. New York: Rizzoli International Publications, Inc.

Simon, Frederick T. 1986. Introduction to accurate representation of surface colors through color graphics. Paper read at Clemson University Computer Color Graphics Conference, 8–9 April, Greenville, SC.

Taylor, Joann M., Gerald M. Murch, and Paul A. McManus. 1988. Tektronix HVC: A uniform perceptual color system for display users. Tektronix Laboratories, Beaverton, OR. *S.I.D. Digest* (Society for Information Display), May 24–26, 77–80.

Verity, Enid. 1980. *Color Observed*. New York: Van Nostrand Reinhold.

Chapter 4

Electronics as a Source of Color

G ood painters understand both how to use their pigments and of what they are composed. The electronic colorist must also know something of the computer in order to maximize its capabilities and to exploit the potential of its color in a creative way.

The color that a computer is capable of displaying is determined by the characteristics of its color monitor. Of course the computer must have the power and appropriate software to produce good color images, but unless the monitor provides adequate color capability, most of the potential for good color graphics that the computer may possess is lost.

COLOR IMAGES

The use of monitors is relatively new to computing. In the ancient computer history of the 1950s, information was put into a computer with punch cards and pulled out from the spool of an automatic typewriter. Now there are many choices for entering information, and many ways in which processed information is returned. A graphic image can be created on a computer using any number of devices. Most of the illustrations in this book were created by typing on a typewriterlike keyboard. It is possible to "type" a graphic image; you need only imagine a piece of graph paper with each line numbered. When you type the numbers of two lines, one horizontal and the other vertical, the location of a particular point is identified. These numbers are stored and remembered by the computer. An individual with the ability to locate one point on the computer possesses the key to an extraordinary drawing instrument. Two points can become a line, and lines can combine to become polygons—with this simple knowledge shapes of every imaginable configuration can be drawn. It is the endless variety of polygons that is of interest to the electronic colorist. By enclosing an area and defining its border geometrically, any polygon on the computer screen can be flooded with color. Colored lines can carry a notational message (the furniture is in red, the walls in blue, for example), but the full richness of electronic color is to be found in the solid color of the filled polygon.

There are other ways to put graphic information into a computer in addition to typing. Electronic pens and wands simulate the feel of a traditional pencil in the hand, giving the sensation of "doing a drawing." The movements of the hand can be captured electronically by moving any number of devices. Regardless of the method used to convey information, each point in a graphic composition is recorded by the computer as numerical data. This "list" of numbers is the graphic composition, but it exists as a picture only when the numbers are called upon to generate an image.

Interactive Drawing

The quickest and most common way to see the graphic information that is stored in a computer is by viewing it on a monitor. On this device the coded visual information becomes a graphic composition for the first time. Unlike the image on a television screen, the computer picture is the invented image of its designer, a plastic image that can be shaped and changed, an image that is alive and capable of responding to further information. Like a drawing on paper, it can be modified at the will of the designer, who is free to react interactively with it. For the designer, this image becomes the created object, the focus of design attention.

This ability to create from the mind and manipulate on the screen is what distinguishes computer graphic images from television pictures. Television produces a photographic recording of what is seen by the camera, an existing view. But graphic images are not photographs, they are an imagined picture, an image from the mind of the designer that has been committed to the computer by movements of the hand. Like drawings on paper or canvas, computer images are the result of an intellectual process that can be controlled and manipulated by their maker.

This manipulation of the computer screen is an entirely new experience for most colorists. Color is handled in a different way. While pencils have long had their erasers and inks their eradicators, changing a color decision has never been an easy process. When transparent watercolor is used, the application of a layer of color represents an irreversible decision; to make a change is to redo an entire drawing. With oil painting or any of the opaque color media, limited changes are always possible, though the spontaneous quality that so frequently characterizes a good drawing can disappear quickly with too many changes. More important, the original colors are lost in the process of making a change and comparisons are not possible.

In most architectural offices, as in schools, it is common to hear of someone "coloring their design." Because of the difficulty of adding color to the usual presentation techniques, color is thought of as something that is added to the design, a final process that brings reality to a designed building. Often the coloring of a project is done as part of an effort to "sell" the design, usually by surrounding it with blue sky and green grass in order to present the design in a familiar environment. The color of a building, if it is included at all, becomes too easily dictated by the colors of the available pencils, rather than by considerations of color itself.

If color is to be considered an element of design, then the coloration of the design should be developed simultaneously with its form.

With computer techniques for coloration, this has finally become a possibility.

Color Processing

The colors that appear on an electronic monitor can be endlessly modified. The digital information that determines a form's color is stored in the computer memory in a file separate from the information that determines shape and size, so changes in color do not affect the appearance of an object in any way other than its coloration.

This is unique to computer drawing. In other media, color must be applied directly to the picture, making the color an inseparable part of the drawn form. The ability rapidly and flawlessly to modify color decisions provides an entirely new graphic process, a technique that could be called *color processing*.

Conceptually, color processing is similar to word processing—a procedure that is accepted by writers everywhere. The use of word processing techniques has revolutionized the role of the secretary in business offices, and it is changing the way that everyone writes. From the first compositions of students in elementary school to the most scholarly of literary pursuits, writers everywhere have been freed from the dominance of their first impulse. No longer must you weigh the costs of retyping against the benefits of a more crafted word; now what is written can be reconsidered, modified, and enhanced without the labor-intensive process of redoing what was already correct. Word processing may be creating a new written aesthetic as the written word becomes electronically crafted.

The electronic colorist can process color decisions in the same way that words are processed. A graphic composition is recorded on the computer as a file of numbers—digits that record each point in the composition and digits that define which points are to be connected with lines. This file can quickly be brought to the screen for review or change.

Color information is usually in a separate file that may be edited exactly as words are edited. When it is desirable to compare two colorations, separate files can be created for each color scheme. Should the color information be a part of the graphic file on a particular system, the entire file can be quickly copied so that two colorations can be developed and compared.

The way color information is given to the computer depends on the computer system being used, both hardware and software. Typically a shape on the screen, a polygon, is identified by typing its number or by pointing to it with some device. The color must then be specified. If it is not to your liking, it can instantly be changed. Usually it is possible to see a list of all the colors to be used in a composition. This list can be changed; you can point to shapes in a composition and ask that they be colored with a particular color. The selection then immediately appears on the screen.

The exact method of color specification used depends on the color model that is used by your equipment. Rudimentary systems use RGB specification, quantifying the amounts of red, green, and blue light needed to produce each color. Technically this is the simplest method for modeling color, though you will find it the most difficult model to picture or to use. Specification by identifying hue, lightness, and saturation is far preferable to naming the RGB values, for it is based on a color model that can be visualized and committed to memory. You must be aware of the potential pitfalls in using HLS color space by anticipating irregularities and compensating for them; in selecting colors, there is no better judge than the human eye. (The available color models are discussed in Chapter 3.)

Picture Units

The computer monitor has a picture tube very much like that of a television set, though of a much finer quality. On the surface of the tube is a grid of very small electronic dots called *pixels* (picture elements). Each dot is a minuscule point of *phosphor,* a chemical that when charged electrically will emit light. The dots are arranged in rows *(rasters)* near the face of the tube in an orderly fashion. The number of dots in a row, plus the number of rows, determines the resolution of the monitor; *resolution* is a measure of the fineness of image it will produce. Television monitors in America have 300 pixels in a row, and require 525 rows to form a television image. It is possible to create graphics with considerable color interest using this degree of resolution, though a resolution of about 1000 × 1000 pixels is desirable to produce a good color graphic image on the screen. This standard is acceptable for most purposes (Mitchell 1987, 35).

At the far end of the picture tube is an electronic gun that fires beams of electrons at each pixel, in a very selective way. As each dot is activated by a stream of electrons from the gun, it emits a light from the phosphor. The dot will glow for as long as it is activated by electrons. An image on the face of the tube is formed by illuminating some of these dots, while leaving others dark.

The computer enters into the graphic process by controlling the stream of electrons, illuminating or leaving dark the various pixels according to the information recorded in the graphic file being drawn. With a black and white monitor, a monochrome image will appear on the face of the tube in the color of the phosphor used, usually white, green, or amber. If the image is to be in color, then the tube becomes more complex.

THE COLOR MONITOR

When the image on a monitor screen is to be colored, the technology that supports it is far more intricate. A color monitor is really three picture tubes in one: The dots that form the pixels on a monochrome screen are triplicated in the color monitor. Each pixel contains three separate dots of phosphor, a red dot, a blue dot, and a green dot, arranged side by side so that each color can be seen simultaneously. The color of a pixel is changed by turning on and off the phosphors of the pixel. Three electron beams are required to do this, one for each color.

The simplest color monitors can display eight colors, including black and white, as shown in Table 4.1. The display is achieved by turning the dots of phosphor on or off selectively. The color choices available are shown in Figure 4.1. Each dot can be individually con-

Table 4.1. An Eight-Color Display on a Color Monitor

Red	Green	Blue	Result
off	off	off	black
on	off	off	red
off	on	off	green
off	off	on	blue
on	on	off	yellow
off	on	on	cyan
on	off	on	magenta
on	on	on	white

Source: Mitchell, Liggett & Kvan 1987, 40.

trolled to create a line drawing. The available colors are adequate to distinguish between types of lines in a plan or a chart. Areas of solid color, polygons of any shape, can be drawn and filled with color from the list of eight colors. Good drawings are possible using only these colors; they provide the substance for an exploration of primitive graphics, and they adapt well to making charts and graphs. In color, they are a bit like the sticker kits that were a part of many precomputer toy collections. With these kits came an assortment of basic shapes in various colors, so that you could lick the sticky backs and paste together a collage on black paper. The computer is more sophisticated because the designer is not limited to a certain number of shapes, but is free to invent forms. For a serious designer, however, this simple monitor does not begin to offer the palette of color that is necessary for color graphic work of any complexity.

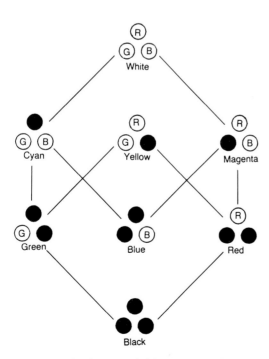

FIGURE 4.1.   The lattice of colors available on a simple color monitor. (Adapted from Mitchell 1987, 41)

The creation of a more complete graphic image requires a larger palette. Many more than eight colors must be available; often thousands or even millions of colors are needed. Having so large a color capacity depends upon two elements that are part of the better graphic monitors: bitplanes and look-up tables.

The Bitplane

A *bitplane* is like a piece of graph paper that has one piece of information, one "bit," at each line intersection; it is a matrix of information that corresponds to the dot pattern on the screen. The bitplane records whether each pixel is turned on or off. If each bit has three colors of phosphor, then three bitplanes are required in the monitor in order to operate the picture tube.

To increase the number of colors available on the screen, the color information that is recorded about each pixel must be increased. A dimmer is required; it is not enough for each dot to be just "on" and "off," it must also be on "low" or "medium" or "high." Then the color choices are enormously increased. Primary colors can be mixed in different proportions, making many more combinations available at each pixel. To accomplish this, more information is needed and more bitplanes are required. Table 4.2 indicates the mathematics of adding bitplanes to a monitor and the corresponding choice of colors that this produces (Mitchell 1987, 37–42).

Eight bitplanes for each of the three primary monitor colors has become a standard and will provide an ample palette for good color graphics. Over 16 million colors can be generated this way. With this equipment, a blending of colors can be achieved similar to that used in painting and in air-gun techniques. The person who must pay for this monitor is often overwhelmed by the number of colors required, though experience will support that need if the colorist is not to be restricted in the use of color. Anyone considering the purchase of a color monitor with less capability should examine samples of the graphics various monitors produce before making a decision.

The Look-up Table

The *look-up table* is a method of shortcutting the number of bitplanes needed in a monitor, while still providing the desired number of

Table 4.2. Total Number of Colors Available at a Monitor

Planes/Gun	Levels/Gun	Available Colors
1	2	8
2	4	64
3	8	512
4	16	4,096
5	32	32,768
6	64	262,144
7	128	2,097,152
8	256	16,777,216

Source: Mitchell, Liggett & Kvan 1987, 42.

screen colors. The effect of having a look-up table is to provide an extensive color palette, but to restrict the number of colors that can be used at any one time. With a look-up table, the monitor can make a large number of colors available, though not simultaneously. This affords a reasonable compromise for the colorist. While it is desirable to select from 16 million samples, very few situations require the use of so many colors at one time.

Monitors are available that provide 256 colors simultaneously through the use of look-up tables from a palette of over 16 million colors (Mitchell 1987, 35–42). This type of monitor has been used for the majority of graphic illustrations in this book. Situations do develop where this is restrictive, particularly in developing color ramps, or in the techniques for producing photorealistic images that simulate the real environment. For many applications, however, it appears to provide an adequate color capacity.

Figure 4.2 illustrates a *gamut chart* that has been drawn on a monitor with a limit of 256 simultaneous colors. The chart shown contains over 1,700 color samples; the photograph is the result of six time exposures made of six separate monitor images onto a color film. Such a chart is a useful graphic device for establishing color standards across the spectrum. Here it illustrates the number of different colors that can be involved in a graphic image. Very few monitors have the color capacity needed to draw this chart in its entirety.

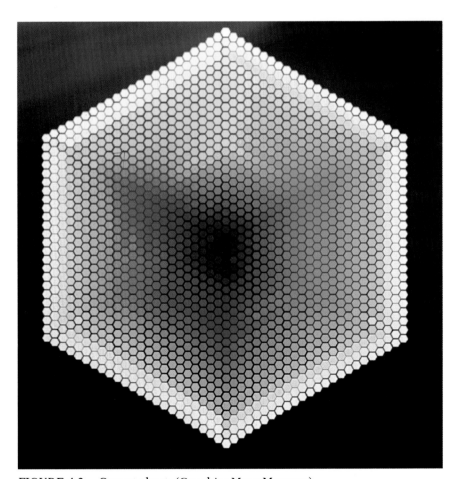

FIGURE 4.2.   Gamut chart. (Graphic: Marc Mascara)

ADDITIVE AND SUBTRACTIVE COLOR

The color on a computer monitor is produced in a way that is new to the graphic artist because it is formed with light. The process begins with a dark screen and gradually adds colored light to it. This is called *additive color* because one begins with the black of the screen and adds color to it; it is the opposite of painting on white paper. In doing a painting, pigment is added to a white surface in order to block a part of the visible spectrum from being reflected; this is called *subtractive color*. The difference is made clear by two illustrations adapted from the work of Josef Albers; Figure 4.3 begins with a dark surface and adds light; Figure 4.4 begins with a white surface and progressively

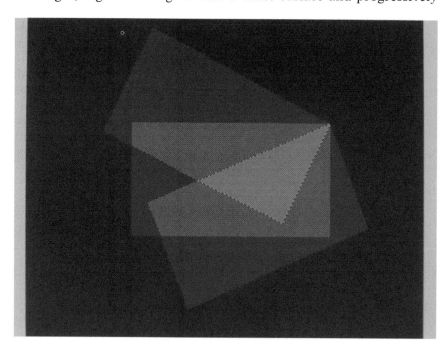

FIGURE 4.3.   Additive color. Computer adaptation from a design by Josef Albers. 1963. (Graphic: the author)

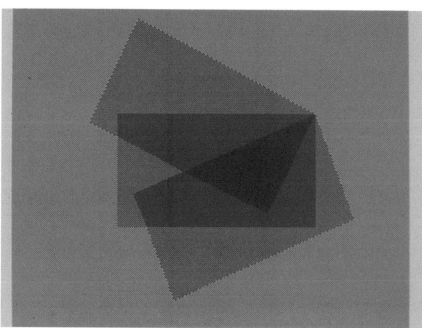

FIGURE 4.4.   Subtractive color. Computer adaptation from a design by Josef Albers. 1963. (Graphic: the author)

removes light. While both images can be computer-drawn, they illustrate the difference between the additive and subtractive processes.

Historically, artists have seldom had the opportunity to use an additive process. Additive color is known mostly in theater lighting, or through the design of stained glass. The result of mixing colors additively can be very different from what is achieved through subtractive mixing. Figure 4.5 indicates the three primary colors of a computer monitor and how they mix additively to form the secondary hues. If these same colors were mixed subtractively, they would appear as shown in Figure 4.6; here the mixed colors are all the same in hue as before, though they are different in value; saturation levels stay the same in each case. Probably the most astonishing discovery for

FIGURE 4.5. Primary colors with additive secondary colors. (Graphic: the author)

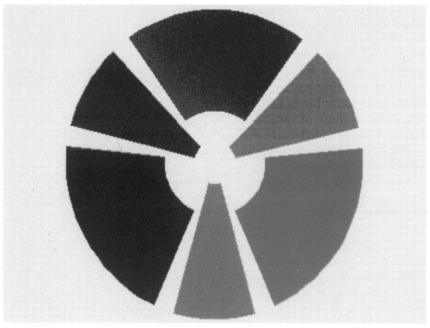

FIGURE 4.6. Primary colors with subtractive secondary colors. (Graphic: the author)

anyone new to additive mixing is to see that the combination of red and green make yellow. Yellow is always the result of this combination, though in subtractive mixing the value is so dark as not to be recognized as yellow. The difference between addition and subtraction is really one of value; additive mixtures are always lighter than their mixture parents, subtractive mixtures are always darker.

Color in Painting and Printing

In printing color pictures for magazines or for books such as this, four colors of ink are used: black, magenta, yellow, and cyan. These inks produce the widest possible range of colors. Printing in color, like painting a picture, is a subtractive process.

A painting usually begins with a piece of white paper or canvas, because white reflects all the colors of light. When you apply paint or ink to paper, you remove from the surface the ability to reflect some of the colors. If the ink is black, then where it is printed there will be no light reflected; that portion of the paper will appear exactly as it would appear in a dark room. Reflectance has been subtracted from the surface. Colored inks have the same effect. When you apply red ink to a piece of paper, then red light alone is reflected—red ink has the ability to block the reflectance of all other colors. Colored inks and colored paints are substances that will not reflect any color but their own. They are subtractive media. The act of painting a picture, like the act of printing a picture in this book, is an example of subtractive color mixing.

Black is used in color printing in order to develop the full range of value from white to black. By combining the white of paper with the black of ink, all the colors of the gray scale can be reproduced. Four colors are therefore used rather than three in order to replicate a maximum portion of the color space.

Both hue and saturation are achieved in a printed picture with colored ink. It is an industry standard to use three colors in addition to black: cyan, magenta, and yellow. These colors are chosen because when mixed by subtraction they produce the greatest variety of colors; they are at the extremes of color space. In the printing process, ink is applied as a fine matrix of dots; in painting, the pigments are usually mixed to form the desired color before being applied. The results in painting and in printing are somewhat the same, though the painter has more latitude because more than three colors can be used as a source—more of the color space can be replicated. Both painting and printing are physically the same in that a color sensation is caused by filtering some of the components of white light from view; they are subtractive processes.

Electronic Color

Color is defined as "a phenomenon of light or visual perception that enables one to differentiate otherwise identical objects" (Webster 1988). Without light there can be no vision, for a totally dark room knows no color. If you gradually admit light into a darkened space, the objects within it are made to appear; they are perceived only because they have color.

Light is called white when all the colors are present. Newton proved this by taking white light and breaking it down with a prism into its component colors (see Chapter 3). Seen through the prism, white light becomes a rainbow of colors, red, yellow, green, and blue, as it is broken into its component parts. White light is composed of all these colors; white is the presence of all color. Black is the absence of all color.

A computer monitor mixes color *additively*. It uses three lights as sources of color: red light, green light, and blue light. Neither black nor white are required as color sources for additive mixing. The picture tube is black until it is activated; white can be achieved by the addition of the colored lights. The particular colored lights that are used have been selected so that in combination they form white light. When you look at a white shape on the picture tube, you are seeing the additive combination of these three light sources.

It is a curious fact that the colors used as primary colors on the computer, the red, green, and blue primaries of additive color mixing, exactly complement the cyan, magenta, and yellow of the subtractive process used in printing. The additive primary colors are the complements of the subtractive primary colors. These six primary colors, three additive and three subtractive, are the colors Frans Gerritsen used to formulate his color model; they are the six primaries of the HVC color solid.

Any of the subtractive primary colors can be seen on a monitor by mixing the additive primaries that bracket the color—yellow by mixing red and green, magenta by mixing red and blue, or cyan by mixing green and blue. This is simply demonstrated with a pair of projectors and slides of each primary color. The same rule holds true for subtractive mixing with paint, although value differences must be taken into account. The muddy-looking brown color that results from the combination of red and green paint is really a yellow. Examine a value-saturation chart and it is there, but we are not conditioned to thinking of yellow in these terms.

THE AUTOMATION OF GRAPHICS

Color manipulation is made simple by the computer, but the profusion of colors can be confusing to a designer. If a portion of the color selection process could be automated without losing control of the color, then automation might be useful. Any process that follows a set of mathematical rules can be written as software for the computer, and many of the operations that consume a designer's time are mathematical operations. When this is the case, the computer should do that portion of the work.

The construction of perspective is probably the outstanding example of a mathematical operation that can be automated, leaving designers free to focus on the other issues.

Perspective

A full-color perspective of a building project is a forceful communication tool. It has a unique and direct way of informing both designer and client of what a design looks like. Perspectives speak in a language that needs no interpretation—they are instantly understood. The construction of perspective drawings is potentially one of the great contributions of computers to the design process, for what was previously laborious becomes instantaneous, labor-free. Once design information is entered into the computer's data base, the construction of even the most intricate perspective can be achieved by this machine. Given ample design information, an abundance of perspective views can be developed by computer. The availability of quick, computer-drawn perspectives is changing the way both designers and clients view their achievements.

The mathematical rules of perspective that were discovered in the Renaissance can now be built into computer software. The information needed to construct a perspective, the three-dimensional geometry of a design, is the same information needed to draw plans and elevations. But there are differences in architectural software: If the location of elements is recorded only in plain view, then the computer must determine heights. When this happens, control of both size and proportion is relinquished by the designer. But if the geometric data is indicated three-dimensionally to the computer, then this same information can be used to draw plan, elevation, isometric, or perspective projections of the design.

To draw a perspective, whether by computer or by hand, you must establish where you are standing by designating a station point; you must also give directions as to where to look, and establish a point that is to be the center of the view. The rest of the construction is just the repetition of mathematical rules and is achievable by machine, resulting in a line drawing similar to that in Figure 2.2. Drawings like these are called wire-frame perspectives because they look as if they were sculpted with wire. The most difficult part of the construction for the computer is the removal of hidden lines. *Hidden lines* are those lines that, because of the transparency of the construction, are seen through what is intended to be solid form. The mathematics of removing hidden lines can be programmed, though the process is intensive in both computer time and memory.

Filling the polygons described by this construction with color creates a colored perspective that obviates the need for eliminating hidden lines. Computer color being opaque, the foreground forms will obliterate the objects behind them, resulting in a full-color perspective that in computer terms is known as a *solid model*. Properly done, a solid model perspective can be a remarkable tool for understanding the physical nature of what has been designed.

Visually, a color perspective is only as appealing as the colors selected for its presentation. While the construction of perspective is automatic, the selection of colors that will give proper definition to form and space is not so easily automated. If a perspective is to be rendered as a solid model, then color must be selected for everything that is seen. This is done by the designer, though again there are several ways that computing can help.

Shade and Shadow

One of the more persistent traditions to come from the Ecole des Beaux-Arts is a technique for rendering shade and shadow. The rendered drawings for which this school is so noted are illuminated by a sun that is assumed to be shining over the designer's shoulder as he draws every elevation, every perspective. The effect of this sun is to cast shadows, as the real sun would cast shadows, on the face of the construction. The result is an understandable, perhaps even joyful, interpretation of the built form that is achieved by definition of shade and shadow. Figure 4.7 illustrates the technique.

When the sun shines on an object, the surface that faces the light source (tangent to it) is the most brilliantly lit. The opposite surface, on the back side of the form, is said to be in shade, for it receives no light, or rather only reflected light. Where shadows are cast, then the surface that receives the shadow is in shadow, and this is the darkest area of all. Those spaces in sunlight that are at angles other than tangent to the sun receive light in varying degrees, depending on their angle to the sun. This rendering of sunlight, shade, and shadow, establishing their proper value differences, is capable of computerization once the color of the original object and the desired degree of value contrast have been established. Rendered in this way, the form is perceived by color definition, following what Johannes Itten described as *contrast of value* (Chapter 2).

FIGURE 4.7.   *A Central School of Fine Arts.* Franklin A. Bermingham thesis, MIT, 1918. (Courtesy of The MIT Museum, Cambridge)

The color of shadow is not so easily determined as that of shade, for it is dependent not on the color of the object illuminated, but on the color of the object receiving its shadow. When light falls on an object, the image of that object is projected through space until the next solid object is found; there it leaves its image. This is the principle of the classical shadow puppet show, and it is also useful in the rendering of form. In a rendered elevation or perspective, the shadows that are cast assist the eye in understanding the three-dimensional quality of the composition.

An underlying principle behind Beaux-Arts drawing is that *shade is rendered half as dark as shadow*. It is a good rule of thumb, and its application will result in believable drawings that simulate well the conditions of a beautiful sunny day. It was an easy principle to practice in the Beaux-Arts, where most structures were conceived in one monolithic material—stone. It is a simple principle to apply to black and white renderings, one that can be verified as fairly valid by studying black and white photographs.

It is more difficult to determine shade and shadow values in color renderings, though rules of thumb can also be applied. If you have committed a color model to memory (see Chapter 3), then you understood that value changes occur along a vertical line passing through color space. Once the hue and saturation of an object are determined, that vertical line is located. The *true* color of an object is the color that it appears in shade. Bright sunlight will cause it to appear lighter; casting a shadow on it will darken it. The rule of thumb, then, is first to identify the color of the object, its hue and saturation, then to select values for sunlight and for shadow that are equally spaced up and down from the point of true shade in color space. In doing this you must be aware of the fallacies of most color solids and make proper adjustments.

Color renderings are an accepted accoutrement of architectural practice today. These renderings, sometimes drawn in tempera paints, though more often with casein or acrylic color, can be largely rendered from three bottles of paint—one for sunlight, one for shade, and one for the shadow value of each material used in the design. These drawings communicate well; properly drawn, they become an effective sales tool for architects. By using the computer, these drawings are the routine product of design studies, a presentation of design ideas for both designer and "designee." But to accomplish colored perspectives, the principles of shade and shadow must be understood and applied by the designer or the computer. Adequate color choices could be made by a computer automatically once the "shade point" of each material was determined. In the use of automatic shade programs, however, a designer should insist on having the ability to override what is "automatically" determined; much of the value contrast in an image is determined by the rendition of shade and shadow.

The Color of Light

The color quality of form changes from "sun point" to "shade point" to "shadow point." A presumption that this is a vertical progression of values assumes that the source of light is a perfect white. This is, of course, not often the case. Sunlight is warm, a color from the warm half of the color solid; as coloration changes from sunlight to shadow it also moves from warm to cool, a fact that many artists have chosen to exaggerate in developing images based on what Itten calls *cold–warm contrast*. In the search for design assistance from the computer, it would be wrong to deprive a designer of such options. Figure 4.8 indicates a wall where vertical value changes are selected; Figure 4.9 uses a much cooler blue tone for shadow. The quality of light is

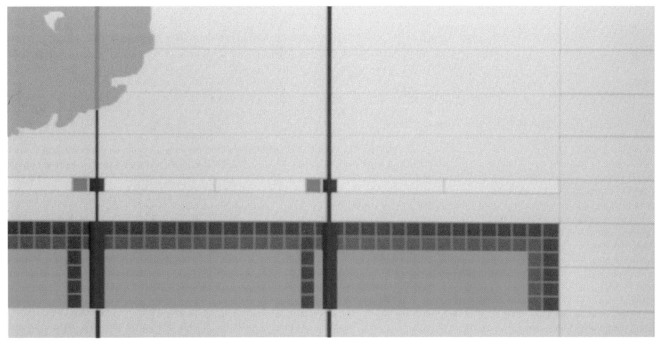

FIGURE 4.8.   Sunlight and shadow as a linear progression of value. (Graphic: David Owen Loy)

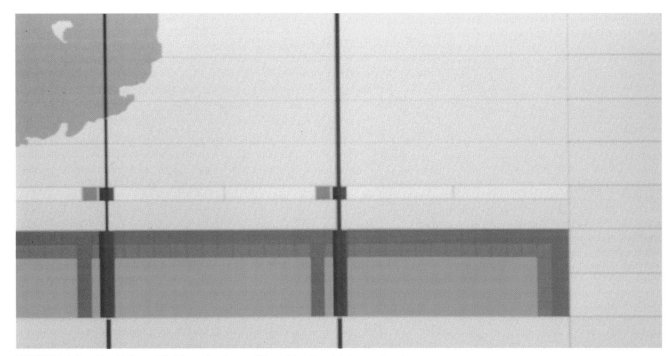

FIGURE 4.9.   Sunlight with blue shadows. (Graphic: David Owen Loy)

conveyed to us in the ways that these shade and shadow tones are rendered.

Light sources produce a great variety of colors. The appearance of an architectural interior changes depending on the color of its illumination far more than its exterior. Interior designers are aware of the differences between tungsten lamps and fluorescent light, halogen light, or the color of sunlight as it passes through tinted windows. The color of a light source is as important to a design decision as its location or brightness. As better computer procedures develop, designers may be able to anticipate the effects of light in their drawings and to respond better to the differences caused by the changing qualities of light.

Color Ramps

A *color ramp* is not really a ramp, but rather a series of even steps that make a transition from one color to another. It is called a ramp when the steps are short enough that they appear to be a continuous blend of color. The gray scale, for example, is a color ramp, a blend of color from white to black. In a color model, if you draw a ramp from white to black in four steps (white, light gray, dark gray, black), then each step is clearly visible and it is not really a ramp at all. If instead you make this transition in forty steps, the drawing will appear as a ramp because it is seen by the eye as a continuous transition of color from one pole to another.

Color ramps can be created between any two colors in color space. For the computer, this is a simple computation; proper hue, value, and saturation levels are calculated for each color sample and rendered in a linear progression between the two colors. If the computer uses a uniform color space, a good ramp is achieved. Many paint programs that define colors by creating ramps are available for computers. The designer identifies two colors in color space, after which the program generates a ramp of color between them. Any point on a ramp is a specific color that can be "painted" on the computer screen. You must be somewhat cautious about what color space is being used by the computer; as we pointed out in Chapter 3, erratic and uneven color changes can be the result of the particular color model. But you can usually compensate for irregularities in the colors you select for rendering if you are aware of the model's weaknesses.

Ramps play a crucial role in the development of computer color graphics. On a screen with a fine resolution and with many color choices, they become a tool somewhat like a watercolor wash—a means of varying color—though unlike watercolor they are a linear progression of colors that cannot easily be arranged in many directions. Properly used, ramps can assist in developing the contrasts needed for a successful composition.

In programming software to generate shading automatically, the color ramp is a useful tool. If the surface of an object faces the sun, then its color is a light value; if it takes away from the sun, it is dark. By defining the "sun point" as one end of a ramp and the "shade point" as the other, a series of colors is generated that responds to all the potential surfaces of the form. If a rounded form is rendered in these colors, it is given a three-dimensional appearance; it lacks only shadows in order to appear as a fully rendered object. A cylinder or a sphere can be rendered like this, and if the ramp is divided into fine enough steps, the surface will appear to be smoothly rounded; if the definition of the ramp is in big steps, the form will appear faceted, but nonetheless offering a graphic indication of the intended form.

In most cases, thirty-two steps in a color ramp will provide adequate steps so that the color transition appears continuous across the face of a rendered object. Automatic shading systems, based on thirty-two-step ramps, will shade each object in a composition with good results, producing a smooth transition from color to color (Van Norman 1988). If there are several million colors available at the same time, this can be an effective way to develop shading. If the system is limited to 256 colors at any one time, this puts severe limitations on the designer, because mathematically there are only seven hue choices available at a time ($7 \times 32 = 224$ simultaneous colors). Effective graphic presentations often involve far more than seven colors.

A color ramp defined by a computer should form a vertical line through a logical color model if the coloration is to follow convention. Not all models are based on a perceived uniform color space; occasionally, the software will produce a color ramp between an identified color and black. The results can be effective, but they neither simulate realism nor give the designer control of the visual effect. Often the software permits both ends of a ramp to be selected, leaving the computer to define even steps between the two points. While this provides better color control, it is less automatic in achieving predictable color results, and requires a good color knowledge on the part of the designer in order to be used effectively. The method of defining color ramps strongly affects the value contrast of a screen image and therefore the quality of the image.

Automatic shading through the use of color ramps can be a tremendous asset to a designer already overwhelmed by the color choices of a typical project. It is one more way that computation can assist the design process. In using automatic shading software, the choice of hue, saturation, and of the "shade point" should be made by the designer. There should be no "default color," no computer-determined fallback for the individual who does not want to make color choices; these are not times to paint the world a standard color! But after a designer has made appropriate color choices, the selection of the values for shade could be left to technology.

Photorealistic Imaging

Enormous progress has been made in recent years toward simulating the real world on the computer screen; the day is not far off when it will take an expert to discern between what is drawn and what is photographed. Automatic drawing of the effects of sunlight and shade on a computer image is all but achieved. Applications of such processes are not hard to imagine, for they will let us look at a completed design before one stone is ever moved. With this ability, visualization of a proposed design can be virtually complete. The difference between reality and imagination becomes ever thinner as we develop more articulate methods of modeling ideas.

Donald P. Greenberg, Professor of Computer Graphics at Cornell University, defines a careful five-step pipeline for creating realistic computer graphic images (Greenberg 1989, 166–167):

1. *The three-dimensional model.* In the first step the geometry of an environment to be modeled is fully defined by the designer; every form, natural and man-made, must be located geometrically. To be complete, the information must include the color and texture of each object, and the color and location of each light source.

2. *Perspective information.* The computer must know where you wish to stand and where you wish to look, in order to generate the desired view. To do this a picture plane is located—the particular surface between the eye and the object on which you wish the image drawn.

3. *Visible surface determination.* Once you have provided the information asked for in the first two steps, the computer determines what is to be seen and throws away the rest of the information. This is an automatic function of good imaging software.

4. *Color determination.* Knowing the color of objects and of the light sources that illuminate them, the appearance of each surface from a particular viewpoint is calculated by the computer. This also is a function of either the hardware or the software. But the computer is only plotting how objects will appear with these particular lights, in this particular position—you, the designer, have determined the color of the objects in step one.

5. *Image display.* After all the calculations have been made, the image is stated in terms of pixel technology. By using this information, a picture may be generated on the screen.

The computer's ability to perform these complex calculations is being refined and perfected. Though historically the fourth point, color determination, has been a major concern of painters, this is not a decision for the electronic colorist working in a photorealistic environment. Such matters can be calculated to achieve realism if the physical description of the object is complete. The considerations involved in this calculation are enormous when one considers the variables of hue, lightness, and saturation on each pixel of the image. The effect of haze on distant mountains must be predicted as it alters hue, and as it reduces saturation. The effect of each color on every other color must be predicted, for the color of every object is in part a reflection of its world. The "interaction of color," to use Josef Albers's words, ceases to be the judgment of the colorist in graphic presentation. But the selection of colors to interact remains beyond science and beyond computers. This selection of color is, and should remain, the decision of the designer.

What is the true color of an object? We have very little definition of this in science or art that is useful to the colorist. In a Beaux-Arts definition, true color is the color of an object as seen in shade. More scientifically, the color of an object is a specification of the hue, lightness, and saturation of the light that is reflected from its surface to the eye when the surface is seen, isolated in an environment of diffuse and perfectly white light. Even this is subject to variance, depending on the brightness of the environment and the success in isolating one object from another.

Several computer drawing techniques have been developed in the continuing effort to produce photorealistic images (Greenberg 1989, 170–172). The complex coloration that gives each surface a real appearance is the result of reflections from everything in the environment. In reality, objects are never illuminated from a single source of light. The reflections can all be calculated; the effect of reflected light rays on the color of each surface, while extensive, is not beyond computation. The calculations produce a very realistic view on the monitor, refining the techniques of traditional shade and shadow rendering to produce a photographic illusion of reality.

Ray tracing is the simplest and oldest of these techniques. It is relatively simple because it is involved with only one view. After a perspective is drawn, the picture plane becomes a computer screen as light rays are traced from the eye's viewpoint, through the complex geometry of reflections to the original light source. The result of these calculations in a definition of red, green, and blue intensity for each pixel in the picture plane, suggesting dots of color not unlike those painted by Seurat (Figure 5.5). The colorist need not be concerned with these calculations, for they are all handled automatically by the software.

Radiosity is a more complex method of achieving these calculations, one that taxes the capacity of today's computers. It is not dependent on any particular perspective, but rather calculates the entire color environment of a composition (Greenberg 1989, 171). Using radiosity, the surfaces of the environment are broken down into patches, or small pieces. The relationship between each patch is then geometrically established; its ability to emit or reflect light is quantified. Solving the mathematics of this relationship is done by the computer; calculations are made for each of the basic colors to determine the correct color of the patch.

The size of the patch involved in a radiosity study depends on the objectives of the study. If the goal is to simulate absolute realism, then, like the pixels of a fine-grained picture, each patch must be small. Realism demands considerable computer memory and the color capabilities of a full twenty-four-bit display monitor. The color information required for these images is enormous (Cohen 1987, 304–306). But the accuracy of a photorealistic image is not always necessary for designers; the spontaneity of a rougher image may well suit their purpose better. This is certainly true in preliminary drawings where considerable design information is simply not known.

As a design is finalized, the methodologies of ray tracing and radiosity analysis can provide excellent design tools. Perhaps their greatest utility comes from their ability to represent light accurately from different sources. By varying the light source, results of color and light decisions can be previewed that before could only be based on conjecture.

Picturing the world in a fully realistic manner is one of the more useful design tools computation can provide. This realism of image, coupled with an ability to select colors for the materials shown, provides a designer with unprecedented opportunity to visualize a design before it is built.

REPRODUCTION OF THE COMPUTER IMAGE

A high-resolution color monitor is the output device of first choice in computer color graphics, for with it a designer can *interactively* relate to a developing design at many levels of sophistication. It is like a sketchbook in that it can capture a thought, and that thought can be changed at will. There is often a closeness, almost a mutual dependence that develops between operator and screen as the computer monitor becomes a new version of the old drafting table.

A color monitor is not the preferred instrument for presentation, though sometimes it is used to present a project to clients in an interactive way. It is limited in both size and portability. But once a color image has been created, there are a number of choices for the presentation of graphics besides bringing a customer to the monitor. The dynamic quality of the computer image is lost, however, once the image moves to any other medium. Like a printout from a word processor, the graphic print captures the ever-changing image at one brief moment in time.

Color Film

To be useful in presentation, a computer image should be available on portable material. In this area color technology is changing rapidly. The greatest sensitivity to the entire gamut of color is currently found in the use of color film. A monitor may be photographed with a quality camera, resulting in good color slides, but a long focal length lens is recommended to minimize the effect of screen curvature. With the use of a tripod in a darkened room and some bracketing of exposures, it is possible to produce excellent quality color slides or photographs of the screen image. The same techniques can be used with video cameras, though the quality of both color and graphics is reduced substantially with most of the cameras currently available.

The majority of the color graphics in this book have been photographed from the computer screen using an *analog* recording camera. This is a device, wired directly to the computer, that photographs the color components of the screen image—red, green, and blue—photographing them one at a time as black and white images on a high-resolution screen. The picture is first photographed through a red, then a green, and finally a blue color filter. Filters are built into the camera to ensure uniform color for each exposure. The entire operation is automatic and results in a triple exposure on color film, yielding a color slide with an excellent resolution of both color and graphics.

Digital film recorders offer many advantages over analog models. We are becoming aware of the difference in sound recording between traditional, analog methods and the newer digital recordings; this same difference occurs in the recording of images. A digital recording camera works directly from the data in the computer—no intermediate monitor is involved. The visual message the recorder receives is therefore first-hand and more precisely controllable; the recorder can even be remote from the monitor, receiving its image by phone or over cables. This equipment provides considerably more opportunity to control the quality and consistency of an image.

But the most difficult of all computer tasks is to maintain consistent color from one device to another. Though one is careful and persistent, there is still considerble variation—color has an elusive quality that is both its joy and its curse. Consistency problems would be helped substantially if the computer industry could agree upon one uniform color space as a standard to which all devices are tuned, but this has not yet happened. Even with identical equipment, there will be differences in the appearance of color from one monitor to another. It is like standing in a television salesroom and examining a wall of receivers—the quality of the color on each one is different. The science of color has much to achieve in this regard.

The frustration of inconsistent color grows as images are printed, but a good process camera provides some control, and color balance can be adjusted to the film being used. Today, with patience, good results and a fair level of consistency are possible.

Color Printers

As a color image is transferred from the computer monitor to the printed page, many changes must take place. The additive coloring of a monitor calls for color definition in terms of red, green, and blue output; the subtractive printing process requires this information in terms of cyan, magenta, and blue. The color gamut, the circle of colors, is like a continuous Japanese fan. One alternately stretches and then collapses its different sides in the never-ending search for balance. Which colors are usually complements? By what criteria? The concept of uniform color space supposes that the space between each color, each leaf of the fan, is equal; but visually equal is not always measurably equal.

The gamut of color is often adjusted by printers in order to obtain a "desirable" color balance. This balance is usually defined in terms of a color spacing that renders good fleshtones in photographs. The color sensitivities of most people demand this. Film companies respond with adjustments that spread some parts of the circle and compress other areas in order to create desirable fleshtones at the expense of other, less noticeable color relationships in the total picture. The position of each color on the wheel, this slight shift in color position due to the balancing process, becomes more critical as we move from additive color to subtractive color.

But despite the problems of color balance, there are astonishing devices being developed for reproducing color images directly on paper. Electrostatic plotters are appearing on the market in larger sizes and with increased color capabilities. These are based on printing in four colors: cyan, yellow, magenta, and black. With software developed specifically for rendering, the red, green, blue, monitor colors are translated to these printer colors (Fisher 1988, 127). The images that these devices produce are improving in clarity and color reliability, and they become less expensive every day.

As equipment comes available with ever larger formats, and at ever lower cost, color becomes more definable and more portable. Both dot matrix and ink jet printers are available, in competition with the electrostatic plotters, and they make use of similar color technology. The full impact of electronic color will probably arrive in the design studios of schools, and in the offices of practicing designers when electronic graphics can be printed in color, simply and economically, in the large dimensions of today's architectural drawings. That day may not be far away.

The ability to transfer color information reliably from place to place is a more evasive problem. A color that is selected by computer in a design office, for example, cannot yet be electronically transferred to the factory where a product is to be manufactured in that color. This challenge requires considerably more color consistency and transferability than is now possible. More important, it will require the acceptance of a uniform color standard to which each device is tuned.

In order to have reliable color transferability, there must be a color space standard, where, after all, would the measurement of distance be if we were still arguing about the length of the meter? Only when every device that produces color is tuned to a uniform standard will color be consistent between devices. If the full potential of computer color is to be realized, then portable color information is a necessary goal; only with such truly interactive color communication can the potential of electronic color be finally achieved.

EXERCISES

1. Slide projectors are excellent instruments for demonstrating color as light. With red, green, and blue slides, using three projectors, the additive combination of primary colors can be demonstrated. You can obtain slides by photographing the computer displays of the colors.
2. Subtractive color mixing can be demonstrated with the same slides used in Exercise 1. Hold several slides together in front of a light to subtract from its whiteness. The mixed results will be very different from what was seen when they were added to the dark screen with projectors.

REFERENCES

Cohen, Michael F. 1987. Radiosity based lighting design. In *Computability of Design*, ed. Yehuda E. Kaley, pp. 303–313. New York: Wiley.

Fisher, Thomas, and Vernon Mays. 1988. The maturing micro. *Progressive Architecture* 69(4):126–31.

Greenberg, Donald P. 1989. Light reflection models for computer graphics. *Science* 244:166–173.

Mitchell, William J., Robin S. Liggett, and Thomas Kvan. 1987. *The Art of Computer Graphics Programming*. New York: Van Nostrand Reinhold.

Van Norman, Mark. 1988. Personal interview.

Webster's Ninth New Collegiate Dictionary. 1988. Springfield, MA: Merriam-Webster.

Chapter 5

The Dynamics of Color

T here is something very inanimate about paint. Given one color and a flat wall on which to apply it, the color of the wall would be as unvarying as painter and paint company could make it—a static surface, void of any suggestion of motion or animation.

Contrast that wall of paint to the green of a forest or the brown of the desert floor and you will see color that is both rich and diverse. A forest is full of trees, each with its own peculiar shade of green. Each leaf is seen to vary, its topside in the sun and full of light, its underside shaded and dark by comparison. There are millions of greens in the forest, each a bit different in hue, each changing in value according to the light it receives, each defined by different degrees of color saturation. So too with the desert floor, where every grain of sand is a different color. We experience in either the forest or the desert a coloration that is dynamic in quality, that is ever-changing as our eyes move and observe each tiny portion of the whole.

DYNAMICS IN PAINTING

A watercolorist could find in the forest or the desert a challenge totally appropriate to that medium. His palette would not contain the millions of colors that are to be seen, but he could find a way to suggest that variation of color. Beginning with a piece of white paper, white because it reflects the entire spectrum of color, he applies his paints. Watercolor paints are really filters for the light that reflects from the paper. If the painter chooses a green, then he selects a pigment that will block all colors except green from wherever it is applied. When we look at his painting, we would experience green reflected from the painted portion of the paper; the experience of all other colors would be filtered out, blocked by the paint (Figure 5.1).

A good watercolorist is adept at finding ways to suggest the richness and diversity of a tree. She understands the dynamic quality of the medium and uses colors well to portray the subject—not millions of colors, but only enough to suggest the dynamics. She wets the paper so that the pigment can mix with water on the paper's surface. She saturates the paintbrush with a lush pigment, suggestive of the darker and richer tones of the forest, and begins a brushstroke across the page. At first the abundant pigment is soaked into the paper, filtering from view all colors except the rich hue. But as the brush moves across the page, the pigment is depleted. An ever-decreasing amount of color mixes with the dampness of the page, and it becomes an ineffective filter. More and more, the other colors of the spectrum are allowed to pass through the filter. We see lighter greens, perhaps yellow-greens or blue-greens; we see decreasing saturations and increasing values of

FIGURE 5.1.   Paul Sawyier. *View of Wapping Street.* ca. 1900. Watercolor on board, 20½″ × 13¾″. (From the museum collection of the Kentucky Historical Society)

color as the ability of the pigment to filter out the other colors is exhausted. In the end we witness a stroke of color that is dynamic, for it presents a different aspect of color to our eye as we observe each portion of the whole. It is this dynamic quality that exists in the best of watercolors, making them animated and appealing to the eye.

The surface of buildings can have a dynamic quality too. One way of achieving this is with texture, when the rough surface of stone or brick is used to reflect light in different ways and to appear as a variety of colors (Figure 5.2). The mosaics of Byzantine churches make use of colored tiles to create images that animate the walls. These walls have a dynamic quality because of the images. When we observe a mosaic we are not aware of the multiplicity of colors, but respond to the dynamics of the surface. The wall seems to animate the entire church, to bring an ever-changing quality as we experience the architecture. The same could be said of Gothic churches, where the colors of stained glass windows fuse in the distance to suggest a common color. From the diversity of this glass comes a rich animation that enlivens and constantly changes the surface of the building. These churches, like all really good architecture, seem to change constantly depending on where you are standing.

Dynamic color changes can also be used to enliven an otherwise flat surface. When an art medium is opaque—that is to say, based on opaque pigments—it is necessary to blend or to contrast colors on the surface of the painting in order to achieve a color dynamic. Oil-based paints adapt well to these techniques, as do casein, tempera, and acrylic colors. When you use opaque color, a variety of color must be applied to the surface in order to achieve what the watercolorist could suggest with one stroke of the brush. If we put a photospectrometer to the human face, we find that the tone of flesh is composed of hundreds of colors. The skin of the woman in Figure 2.17 is painted with many colors that combine dynamically in order to model the tone of her

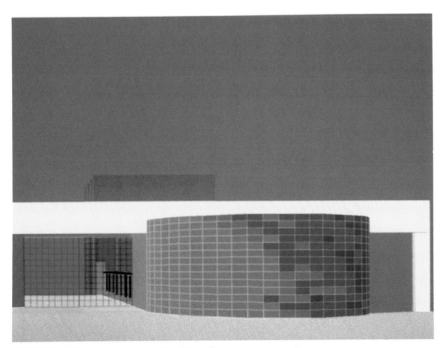

FIGURE 5.2.   Textured wall. (Graphic: Jerry Hupy)

flesh. Though not noticeable at a casual glance, her face is an intensely saturated purple. The color, however, appears quite natural; the palette has shifted dynamically to recognize and reflect her surroundings.

IMPRESSIONISM

Advances that were made in chemistry in the nineteenth century enriched the palette of the artist with an abundance of new pigments. These new colors were more intense in hue, capable of producing a brilliant coloration in paintings. When impressionist painting began about 1830, several fresh approaches to coloration took advantage of these new pigments. Many techniques now applicable to the electronic palette were first used by the impressionist painters.

The era of impressionism was probably the greatest time for experiment in the use of color in recent history. Impressionist paintings possess a dynamic quality that to a large extent accounts for their continued popularity. Impressionists focused more on the use of color as a design element than had artists who followed earlier styles or movements. For the electronic colorist, the lessons of impressionism are many. The use of atmospheric haze as an abstraction to imply depth comes from impressionism. Edouard Manet, for example, explored the use of color to augment mechanical perspective as a depth-giving device. Foreground objects in his paintings were rendered in relatively saturated color, while those in the background disappeared into an exaggerated atmospheric haze. His paintings of the great nineteenth-century railroad stations articulate steam engines in the front of the station using strongly contrasting values, though the perspective of the shed is lost in an atmosphere of steam.

Of all the impressionist painters, Claude Monet was most involved with the effects of light on the color of objects. His series paintings of the House of Parliament, or of the Waterloo Bridge, focus on the dynamic quality of surfaces as they change during the course of a day. In his paintings of the cathedral at Rouen, Monet was able to indicate the time of day by the colors selected for each painting. The stones of the church appear re-colored as the sun moves through its course, providing the great cathedral with an ever-changing aspect. In the first light of morning the façade is lit from behind; the sun is in the eastern sky (Figure 5.3). The stones of the church become blue, dark in contrast with the lighter green-blue of the sun-filled sky. There are no shadows to sculpt the form, only the reflected yellow of the sun as it accents the doors and sharpens the profile of the steeples. As the day passes, the stones exhibit an ever-changing color. By late afternoon, the evening sun is directly lighting the great portal (Figure 5.4). Now the stones have turned to a light yellow, seen against the dark purple-blue of the afternoon sky. The doorways deepen to a richer reddish tone in contrast with the weathered stone. These paintings are atmospheric in nature. The surface of the architecture is sculpted not with perspective, but with the qualities of light, which are shown with color.

Monet's paintings are composed of great dabs of juxtaposed pigment that form images of a rich and varied environment. Sometimes these colors join, sometimes they form a spatial separation. Always it is the reaction of one color to another that is the special chemistry of

FIGURE 5.3. *Rouen Cathedral, West Façade;* Claude
MONET; National Gallery of Art, Washington; Chester
Dale Collection.

FIGURE 5.4. *Rouen Cathedral, West Façade, Sunlight;*
Claude MONET; National Gallery of Art, Washington;
Chester Dale Collection.

his paintings, giving them their quality of depth and light. The motion, the animation of the painting is caused by an interaction of color,
sensations that are due to the artist's choice of color adjacencies. The
use of atmosphere as a depth-giving device was familiar to architects
studying at the Beaux-Arts Institute in Paris. The watercolor washes
that have become their hallmark depend on intensely detailed fore-
grounds of color, while distant elements were dissolved into a neutral
mist (Figure 4.7).

Georges Seurat, another of the impressionists, brought these attitudes into the twentieth century when he reduced the application of
color to a series of tiny dots, anticipating modern color printing processes and demonstrating the ability of the eye to blend many colors
into a harmonious image. *Sunday Afternoon on the Island of La Grande
Jatte* is a huge painting which, viewed from 30 feet away, has a very
realistic appearance. Only on close inspection do the individual dots
of color become apparent (Figure 5.5). Each speck of color has its own

FIGURE 5.5.   Georges Seurat. Detail, *Sunday Afternoon on the Island of La Grande Jatte*. 1884–86, oil on canvas, 207.6 × 308.0 cm, Helen Birch Bartlett Memorial Collection, 1926.224. detail: view #6. (©1989 The Art Institute of Chicago. All Rights Reserved.)

identity on close inspection, but disappears into a unified color image when seen from a greater distance. This same process, on a much finer scale, has been used in the last century for printing colored pictures, and is applied today in forming the picture elements of the color graphic computer screen.

THE ALBERS COLOR DECEPTIONS

For architects, no single event has influenced either the design of buildings or the use of color in the recent past as much as the founding of the Bauhaus in Weimar, Germany, in 1918. The artists of the Bauhaus crystallized the principles of color use that had been so evident in the art of the impressionists. Johannes Itten, responsible for the basic course at the school, formulated a method of study that verbalized a design vocabulary common to the arts. The methods used in his courses have permeated the teaching of architecture, and to some extent the teaching of all the visual arts. Itten's theories on the contrast of color are the topic of Chapter 2 of this book. His pupil and later his colleague, Josef Albers, spent a lifetime probing the behavior of color.

Interaction of Color (Albers 1963) is his definitive treatise on the use of color in design. It is the culmination of a lifetime of the teaching of color that began in the Bauhaus, moved to Black Mountain College in North Carolina, and finally relocated to Yale University. The book is intended as a teaching folio, a collection of work by Albers and his students that systematically explores color interaction. It dramatically demonstrates with over eighty illustrations that the appearance of any color depends on its interaction with adjacent colors. Figure 5.6 is a study for that book by Josef Albers. These are the original silk screen studies for the book. While the studies are beautiful in the hands of their maker and as they appear on the printed page, as print they are an inflexible media for studying color.

For the electronic colorist there is no better teacher of color behavior than a careful study of the plates in *Interaction of Color*. They are for the most part geometric, and as a composition capable of being scaled and replicated on the most rudimentary of computers. Their coloration is a very different matter, requiring both a computer with

FIGURE 5.6.   Josef Albers. *Two Studies for Interaction of Color*. ca. 1961. Silk screen on paper mounted on paper, 20 × 19″ (50.8 × 48.3 cm.) (©1963 Yale University Press. All rights reserved. Courtesy of The Josef Albers Foundation)

an extensive color capability and an operator with a sensitivity to color. These are not easy colors to duplicate; but they are self-correcting, for a wrong color will inevitably fail to illustrate the object of the study.

To duplicate what Albers has illustrated is possible in almost any medium and worthwhile as an experience. By finding his color selections on the computer, we start to sense how they relate both to a system of color and to each other. If the color model used by the computer is logical, then by finding the color it is also identified. The next step toward mastering these color dynamics, selecting your own colors and observing their interaction, is probably best done on the modern color graphic computer. This can become a tedious chore with a less flexible medium, unless you happen to have Josef Albers by your side.

In the classes taught by Albers, colors were usually picked from a large supply of colored papers. These were purchased as packets of printing paper and provided a palette of several thousand uniform color sheets. Alternatively, paper samples were collected by students wherever they could be found. Periodicial collections in the libraries of many an architectural school have been decimated by armies of freshmen, armed with scissors and charged with this project. The modern computer can provide several million colors from which to choose a color palette, and also insure an intact library of periodicals.

At the Bauhaus, a question would be asked by the master, a color "challenge" would be given. Its solution was to be found among the thousands of colors at hand in the large sheets of color arrayed across the floor. In the computerized studio it is still a joy to undertake these exercises, and for many students the tediousness of the process is relieved through the use of computer color.

To Make One Color Appear as Two

This basic Albers exercise sounds impossible; it proves in fact to be simpler than it looks. Color is a fickle commodity and if given a chance, will change faster than a chameleon. The quality of any single color is totally dependent on what surrounds it. Value changes can be demonstrated with only three shades of gray. A middle gray color will look dark on a light gray ground and light on a dark gray ground, providing a rudimentary example of the principle. Expanding this concept to a whole range of grays can produce in black and white a dramatic demonstration of the changing nature of color even when it is represented only by value differences.

Figure 5.7 is a computer drawing, a copy of a composition in which Josef Albers illustrates how a middle gray value can be made to look either light or dark, depending on the values surrounding it. Both the frame around this composition and the line down the center are a single middle gray value that is made to change in its apparent value, depending on which colors are adjacent.

Changes of value are relatively simple to produce on a computer, and the results are usually dramatic; changes in hue or in saturation can be equally dynamic. These deceptions are startling and, given a careful selection of color, produce almost unbelievable demonstrations of a basic principle of color interaction. Albers was a master at

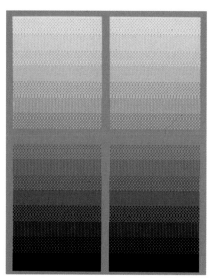

FIGURE 5.7.   Composition of values. Computer adaptation from Albers 1963. (Graphic: Peter Schlossman)

this. He would urge his students to stretch a color phenomenon as far as possible—to create totally unbelievable color diffferences—to turn black into white if they could. Figure 5.8 demonstrates this, changing the diagonal magenta bars to appear as two different values; Figure 5.9 "proves" the composition by removing the middle bars, proving that both sides are, in fact, one color. The ability to "prove" a color phenomenon is an important by-product of computer color. In Figure 5.10 this difference in color appearance is stretched even further, indicating how unbelievably far the appearance of a single color can be distorted.

Changing the hue of a color, or its saturation, is more difficult than changing the value, but follows the same principle. The appearance of a particular hue can shift to the left or the right around the circle of hues in contrast with the ground it is placed upon. It is a bit like stretching a rubber band and as an exercise should probably be taken that way. For example, Figure 5.11 uses a band of color that appears to be green on a magenta ground, and yet magenta when the background is green. The further this color difference is stretched, the more a difference is created between colors and the more unbelievable the demonstration becomes. But there is, of course, a breaking point beyond which color shifts do not work and the effect is lost.

The display on a computer screen is a good place to begin these exercises. If you have good control of the color changes within any given area, you can fine-tune the exercise in a way that would have been totally unavailable to Albers. You can process the color, changing

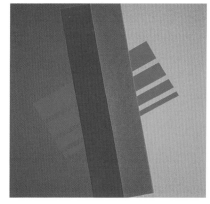

FIGURE 5.8.   One color appears as two. (Graphic: Todd Boggess)

FIGURE 5.9.   Proof that one color appears as two. (Graphic: Todd Boggess)

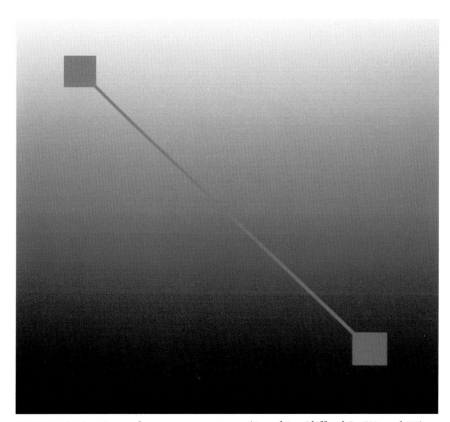

FIGURE 5.10.   One color appears as two. (Graphic: Clifford D. Kinard III)

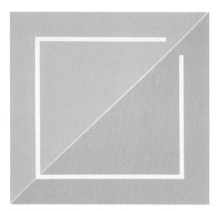

FIGURE 5.11.   One hue can be made to look like two. (Graphic: Gwinn Gibson Harvey)

incrementally the hue, the value, and the saturation until the effect is visually maximized. You can save a color combination, go backward or forward, make any of those changes at which computers are so good. A lifetime of experience with any other medium can be summarized in a relatively short time.

To Make Two Different Colors Appear the Same

If one color can be changed to two, then the reverse must be true; two colors can be changed to one. This is a harder assignment, dependent as much on composition as on color.

In Figure 5.12, two small squares of color are presented, one on a magenta ground and the other on green. These small squares appear to be the same color. But look carefully. What color are they? At the bottom center of the composition the colors of the squares have been reversed. That which was on green is now seen on magenta and proves to be a darker shade of green; the opposite color—originally on the magenta ground—is displayed on green and is now proved to be a shade of magenta.

Relative area and proportion have much to do with achieving success in this exercise. It requires only four colors, two backgrounds and two figures, one to be placed on each ground. Done correctly, one sees only three colors. The figures have been visually changed to appear the same. The more extreme the differences in figure color, the more dramatic the proof of this exercise becomes. Figure 5.13, similar in composition to Figure 5.10, again shows two small squares. This time they appear to be the same color. But check Figure 5.14, where

FIGURE 5.12.   Two colors appear as one. Computer adaptation from Albers 1963. (Graphic: the author)

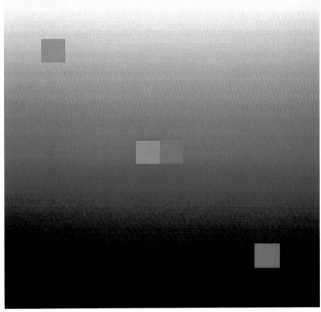

FIGURE 5.13.   Two colors appear as one. (Graphic: Clifford D. Kinard III)

FIGURE 5.14.   Proof that two colors appear as one. (Graphic: Clifford D. Kinard III)

the colors are brought to the center and repeated. Two very different greens have in fact been made to appear as the same color.

The ability to reduce the number of colors in a composition becomes yet another design factor to consider and manipulate. Design choices increase as this is explored, making the computer a useful design tool. The proportion of the parts can be modified or the hue, value, and saturation of colors can be changed; a designer has many choices. If the figure in a composition is too large, then its own identity asserts itself and the two colors are read as separate and distinct. Albers would solve this problem in a number of ways. One direct solution was to cut holes in a large figure to let the background read through (Figure 5.15). The eye should never be permitted to see too much of a figure at one time, or the effect will be lost. No exercise emphasizes the relationship of proportion to color selection as much as the effort to make two colors appear to be the same.

FIGURE 5.15.   Color saturation. Computer adaptation from Albers 1963. (Graphic: the author)

To Lose the Identity of a Color

It is possible to take this color magic further. With a little study, colors can come and go in an Albers composition faster than rabbits at a circus. For example, the identity of a color can be completely lost. Even colors as diverse as complements can be made to appear the same. The XX composition shown in Figure 5.16 illustrates this well. Two Xs are rendered in rather broad lines, side by side and each on a different ground. They appear to be two different colors. In one case the first X is yellow and the second is purple. But look carefully at the composition, for the Xs are joined, ever so subtly, at the top. They are in fact one color. Finding this is generally a moment of discovery. How

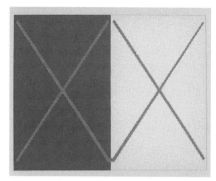

FIGURE 5.16.   Disappearing color. Computer adaptation from Albers 1963. (Graphic: the author)

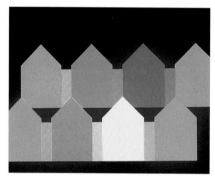

FIGURE 5.17.   Houses. (Graphic: Gustus Fischer)

is it done? It is one of the great riddles that suggest the character and determination of a man devoted to the study of color.

None of these problems can be solved by formula; color by its very nature is too elusive. There always seems to be one more factor that accounts for its misbehavior. But this particular riddle comes closer than most to a calculated solution. If you can specify color on your computer by indicating hue, value, and saturation, then you will have a chance. Select two grounds for a beginning, two very diverse colors. Then determine the averages. Find the average hue, value, and saturation of the two grounds. Color both Xs this color and you will probably find yourself very close to a solution. If it doesn't quite work, try lowering the saturation a bit. If you enjoy mathematics, you can come close to solving this problem much quicker with a computer than you can with paint or with colored paper.

How can color manipulation be applied to design? While the answer comes in many forms, the row of houses shown in Figure 5.17 is based on the same principle as Xs in the previous example. Eight little houses are shown, with a rather nasty array of color selections. The question of how they can be linked is resolved by the color bridges between them. These connecting colors were selected, as were the colors of the Xs, to relate to the adjacent colors. No matter which house you picture yourself in, this bridge will always appear to be the color of the house next door.

The astonishing thing about copying a composition by Albers on the computer is to discover the ease with which it can be done. Part of this can be attributed to the simplicity of processing colors on a computer, the ease with which you can change from one color to another. Another explanation may be that the phosphors that produce electronic color are a more intense color source than that available with pigments. Remember that the color palette available with the standard Munsell color system can be expanded 40 percent using a good color graphic monitor. The availability of perfectly flat planes of color, of an extended color palette, and of the simple means to explore these color interactions creates an exciting new electronic environment for the exploration of color.

There is no mystery to the work of Albers. The color phenomena he demonstrates, making one color appear as two, or making two colors appear as one, or even losing the identity of a color, are all explained in terms of how the eye sees color—the effects of after-image. (For a discussion of after-image, see the section on simultaneous contrast in Chapter 2.)

COLOR DYNAMICS TODAY

Television has not missed the opportunity to utilize color dynamics. Between every program, the station logo appears; at the beginning of every home video is the logo of a distributor. Newscasts in particular involve the use of titles and logos that are color graphic compositions, used to dissolve one image into another, using the color effects that Albers demonstrated to bring life to the flat colors of the computer graphic media. For the colorist, these graphics are often examples of the best current work in electronic color manipulation (Figure 5.18). Many unspoken credits are due Josef Albers for the effects that are obtained. The expertise developed by the television industry in using color dynamics can be applied by architects and designers as they begin electronic presentations of their own work. These dynamic effects can be applied to architecture, both to the presentation of buildings on a computer screen and perhaps even to the buildings they design.

Architects usually present their building designs with pencil or ink sketches, or as drawings done in colored pencil and with bottle markers. When really fine color drawing is required, a professional renderer is often contracted to do the drawing. Traditionally, professional presentations are rendered in casein, tempera, or acrylic paint. They utilize the last vestiges of the careful Beaux-Arts rules for drawing sunlight, shade, and shadow in an architectural rendering. In principle, three colors are mixed in separate bottles for each material in the rendering: a bottle of sunlight, a bottle of shade, and a bottle of shadow. Done well by a caring and practiced hand, these images are magnificant idealizations of how a finished product might look. As sales tools and promotional material, they are successful in giving future owners something they can understand, possess, and utilize until the real building is built.

FIGURE 5.18.   Newsline Logo for WYFF, Greenville, SC. (Courtesy of Digital Images, Editel/Boston)

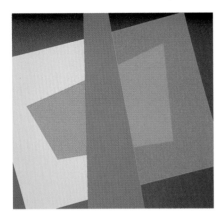

FIGURE 5.19.   One color appears as two. (Graphic: Stephen M. Denton)

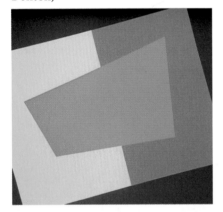

FIGURE 5.20.   Proof that one color appears as two. (Graphic: Stephen M. Denton)

Electronic media could change these methods of presentation. How are the new images to differ from the old reliable drawings? The computer can construct a mechanical perspective in a very short time. It can calculate shadows and offer a variety of environments to provide a setting for the architecture. Much of the pastiche provided by the professional renderer can exist in the computer: background, trees, scale figures, even the color of the buildings if you choose not to pick your own. For a client, these drawings can provide a feeling of being involved with the process because they have the potential for being instantly changed.

For the electronic renderer, the new medium is a challenge. Methods must be found to use flat colors to advantage. One answer is using the simple Albers exercise of making one color appear as two. Figure 5.19 is an abstract design that changes the apparent color of the central form. That it is one form is shown by Figure 5.20. Figure 5.21 explores its application to architectural form in rendering the top of a tower. Here the window openings, all the same color, illustrate a dynamic color change as they appear on different sides of the tower.

The ability of a foreground color to change from one background to another can be a source of dynamics, of movement within a drawing. The ever-changing colored surface is alive and provides interest to a composition. Just as a wall can be made a focal point by providing it with texture or sculpture, so it can be animated by using a changing background. In a rendering, the use of changing colors as background can be a very subtle means of providing greater interest in a drawing.

FIGURE 5.21.   Tower. (Graphic: Stephen M. Denton)

FIGURE 5.22.   The Beach
Apartments by day. (Graphic:
Stephen M. Denton)

FIGURE 5.23.   The Beach
Apartments by night. (Graphic:
Stephen M. Denton)

In a real building this technique becomes more difficult to apply, for the background is ever-changing and thus harder to control. The quality of a building to look different at dawn than at midday, or to be more appealing in sunlight than in a storm, can be explained in part by the naturally occurring background changes (Figures 5.22 and 5.23). With electronic media, these changing backgrounds can be anticipated and colors selected to use the changes to advantage. By understanding the dynamic color shifts that might be anticipated in an architectural element, colors can be selected to maximize the dynamic experience of the building.

Albers has also illustrated how two different colors can be made to appear the same. Properly used, this too is a dynamic tool in architecture. When two backgrounds are different in color, then any common elements can be colored to appear the same. Is there an architectual value in this exercise? Confusion can be reduced, unity can be reinforced. If it were felt to be desirable, then the shady side of a building could be made to read exactly as the side that faces the sun.

FIGURE 5.24.   Two colors as one. (Graphic: Walter Alan Nurmi)

Le Corbusier understood this when he painted the shadows on his Unité d'Habitation Berlin. With the ability for a more finite control of color, we gain better control of the appearance of buildings (Figure 5.24). With electronic rendering, we can easily study these situations. With dynamic color selections, we come to understand that these phenomena will help to illustrate designs to us and to our clients, and to achieve a greater dynamic in our buildings.

It might at this point be fair to ask why in architecture we would want to lose the identity of a color. Often a designer is presented with two discordant objects. These might be a pair of buildings whose colors were never meant to be seen together, but that suddenly need to be linked with a bridge. In painting, this would be somewhat like the still-life painter presented with an apple and an orange who now must find the common ground to unite them in a composition. The solutions that develop from the study of Albers are one way to resolve this problem, but there are no doubt many others.

DYNAMIC ARCHITECTURAL IMAGES

One of the more peculiar qualities of computers is the credibility their images seem to create. People believe what comes from a computer far more than if they are simply told the same information, or shown it in a pencil sketch. Perhaps it is the fact that an expensive machine has accepted some information, applied some mathematical logic to it, and presented it in a very finished way. Most architectural clients today, in fact many architects themselves, believe, respect, and accept a plan printed from a computer as a more perfect object than a hand-produced drawing of the same plan. The colored image that comes out of a computer, if it has an appealing and informing quality to it, is more believable than what is colored by hand. Electronic color will change the way architects see buildings and could change their own thought process as they develop electronic images of the buildings they design.

Variation of surface color, the technique that so often adds richness to a watercolor image, cannot logically be duplicated on a computer; moreover, such pictures are probably not appropriate computer output. Through television we have gradually come to realize the differences between electronic imagery and those of a more traditional medium. Computer graphic images, like television pictures, are not studied in detail. It is a passing imagery that depends upon instant overall recognition of composition. Neither the time allocated for a particular impression nor the detail afforded by the screen permits the careful observation traditionally given a watercolor painting. A new medium requires new methods. Color dynamics provides an alternative to the color variations of watercolor techniques. It uses the flat tones of the electronic media effectively to create surfaces that are dynamic, alive, and moving. Through dynamic coloring, the bold gestures of composition and movement required by the electronic media can be achieved.

What we experience in a rendering, we can also hope to achieve in reality. Only when we are truly in control of an architectural design can we hope to control the changing patterns of figure and ground as we move through a building. With this control comes the opportunity for a lively dynamic design, generated by the surfaces of the building and by the objects within it. This is the greatest challenge of all in applying the dynamics of color to a work of architecture.

EXERCISES

1. Make one color appear as two.
2. Make two different colors appear to be the same.
3. Lose the identity of a color.
4. How can these principles of color interaction be applied; to architecture? Can you use the computer to produce an example?

REFERENCES

Albers, Josef. 1963. *Interaction of Color.* New Haven, CT: Yale University Press.

Chapter 6

Illusions of Space and Form

W hile modern architecture has traditionally concerned itself with the definition of space, current attention is focusing on the importance of form—on the treatment of shape and surface in order to create a sense of place. But whether the issue is the comprehension of drawings or the visual perception of buildings, what we see—what our eyes and our minds read as either space or form—is determined by the color environment of our view. Open your eyes to the world, or to the computer monitor, and you will experience a figure-ground pattern. One group of colors unite to form a figure, an object in front; another group of colors seems to pass behind this figure and form a background to it. Our visual environment is layered with objects in space.

Our eyes are educated to the rules of perspective. The understanding of physical placement afforded by a lifetime of experiencing perspective helps us to distinguish foreground from background. This distinction is clearer when the perspective is well colored, for color has its own vocabulary of depth perception totally aside from the mathematical laws of perspective. Perspective can be achieved with color alone.

TRANSPARENCY

If an object is transparent, then we can see through it in order to discover what is behind. If this spatial placement can be achieved with paint, or with electronic color, then we have achieved the illusion of depth without the aid of mechanical perspective.

> At the Bauhaus Albers had continued his technical explorations and further refined his eye. Eloquence and simplicity of composition are consistently apparent in his work of the period. But around the year 1930 he also immersed himself in visual mischief. For example, he pursued the creation of illusory transparency—a theme he would treat in *Interaction of Color*. . . . He did this by finding the precise tone that would have been created if these shapes were transparent and superimposed. It thrilled the artist to find that art provided experiences that nature could not offer. (Weber 1988, 27)

Josef Albers used transparency, or rather the mental image of transparency, as a way to define space and to experience form. Architectural imagery depends on using this illusionary transparency; by using the device, we are able to see into windows, through windows, out of windows; we are able to see from one place into the place beyond—all the experiences that add to the perception of depth and to the establishment of a sense of place. In the graphic arts, depth within an image can be established by the presumption of a sort of atmospheric haze, through which the objects "beyond" are experienced. It is a classic technique, often used in both architectural presentation and in painting.

Figure 6.1 is a computer drawing, a replication of a composition by Albers. It appears to be a simple drawing, showing four squares of color on which a square of transparent tape has been pasted. The tape seems to be bent, doubling back across itself and over the bottom two squares. As a drawing it is simplistic and easy to duplicate on a computer. To color the drawing, to develop on a computer the proper colors to illustrate this transparency, is far more difficult. Computer colors are opaque; the experience of seeing one color through another requires the use of illusionary transparency. Drawing the composition illustrated in Figure 6.1 on a computer, one must do as Albers has done with his class, or with the screen prints in *Interaction of Color* (Albers 1963). It is necessary to define ten distinct colors. First, four colors are selected for the background; next, knowing that computer

FIGURE 6.1.   Illusion of transparency. Computer adaptation from a design by Josef Albers 1963. (Graphic: Ernest E. Fava, Jr.)

colors are opaque, four more colors are selected that represent these base colors as they would appear when seen through transparent tape; then the composition is completed by selecting two more colors that represent two of the base colors as seen through two sheets of the transparent material. In total, ten discrete colors are needed.

Designers who possess some knowledge of computers are aware that programs have been written that will make the selection of "transparent" colors for you. A number of commercial programs have a function that lets you select *transparent,* and whatever color you draw will appear transparently, rendered on top of the background color. While the development of such software is to be encouraged, we must be cautious here. There are many decisions to be made about the nature of this transparency. Whether made by a designer while producing computer drawings, or by a computer programmer writing color graphic software, a decision must be made as to the appearance of this color.

Most software programs assume that a transparent area should be a color that is one-half white and one-half the base color, perhaps a logical assumption for many uses and certainly one that yields interesting results. But the rendering of transparency is an old and honorable art and the history of art is filled with examples of its use in all manner of ways. The clinging, revealing clothing of classic Greek sculpture has been a favorite painter's topic for a long time. In the drape of the central figure of Grünewald's painting (Figure 2.14), the cloth clings to his body, revealing both itself and the form beneath. The transparency used in this painting is not the simple abstraction of the Albers study, nor is it a subject that could be rendered easily with a transparency formula. This transparency is effective because of the artist's mastery of color, his ability to select colors that articulate the form on top and the form beneath. The colors involved are not beyond the abilities of a computer.

Albers has said that you should close your eyes to see in your mind the image you are trying to color, and then select colors from this imagery; Grunewald himself in all likelihood followed a procedure not too different. If you define each area of color in a composition and then select the proper color for it yourself, your art will be limited only by your imagination; if you rely on the talents of a programmer to provide adequate coloration, then you cede these decisions to someone else.

Of course, it is possible to be analytical about color decisions. You know the color of the background and can assume the color of the transparent material. You can make an assumption as to the degree of transparency desired. Forty percent? Maybe 60 percent? If the material is seen at an angle, then you could develop factors of transparency for that. The techniques would be somewhat like those developed for ray tracing, discussed in Chapter 4. But traditionally you would look at a color and know if it were right or wrong; that is the way colors have always been selected in painting, and there is little in computation to suggest that it should be otherwise.

Another question should be asked here: How much of the perceived transparency in the Albers illustration is due to the fold in the transparent material? If there were no fold, just four background colors and the four colors that are seen through the transparent tape, would the composition so completely convey the designer's intent? It is doubtful that the illusion would be as complete, but if you are unsure, then the computer provides a quick way to find out. Composition is as important to this deception as selection of the correct color.

The significant issue raised by the illustration, however, is not the techniques for achieving transparency; rather, it is the admission of a successful illusion of transparency. To agree that the tape appears, in fact, on top of the four background colors, is to concede that one form (the tape) is seen in front of another (the background); they have become objects that relate spatially. Without any indication of perspective, Albers has succeeded in assigning positions to objects, in locating the forms in space. The composition has become three-dimensional.

PERCEPTION OF SPACE

The definition of space in a two-dimensional drawing is a classic design problem. Whether doing a sketch for one's own use or laying the groundwork for a lavish design presentation, the ability to represent a three-dimensional object on a flat surface is an issue central to design thought and design process. It is the means by which we visualize a design.

Atmospheric Illusion

When we draw a room and see through the window of that room into a space beyond, we have begun an effective composition because we have defined the room as foreground and the scene beyond as background (Figure 2.17). It can be equally effective to look at a building with a considerable amount of glass in its façade, and to see through that glass into the space within the building. In either case, looking out or looking in, the glass is made to modify in some way what is seen in the distance.

Whether one is looking into or out of a window, the use of transparent color to define space by separating foreground from background is an effective device. Figure 6.2 is a simple composition, a view looking through both one and two panes of glass, because the window is partially raised. The buildings seen outside this window are muted as viewed through one windowpane, and muted still further when viewed through two sashes. Figure 6.3 illustrates a more complex use of transparency on the computer, which achieves the illusion of distance through the reflections in a mirror. Distance is achieved by assuming that the reflected color will be modified by the transparent qualities of the reflecting mirror glass; as the image is reflected, the reflections become progressively muted.

The ability of the atmosphere to affect color perception is an effective visual tool. If you have had the opportunity to drive through hilly country, in an area were the countryside displays itself in layers between foreground and sky, you are well aware of the effects of atmospheric haze; you have seen it in the layering of the hills as their color is muted from ridge to ridge. At the right poetic moment on such a trip, the world seems revealed in layers of landscape; each successive layer is transformed in the haze distance provides.

The effects of atmosphere can be exaggerated in a visual presentation. To do this, objects that are farthest in the distance are obscured

FIGURE 6.2.   Cat in a window. (Graphic: David A. Hill)

FIGURE 6.3.   Reflections in a mirror. (Graphic: Lance Jaccard)

FIGURE 6.4.   Elevation. (Graphic: Norman E. Bello, Jr.)

by assuming a semi-transparent environment; they become grayer, less distinct, and less detailed as they are obscured by the thickness of the air through which they are seen. Albert Munsell would describe the process as moving the color toward the center of the color sphere (Munsell 1976)—the color is de-saturated and its value becomes closer to middle gray. Foreground objects are rendered in relatively intense color that exhibit a stronger contrast of value. One should also note the tendency of light colors to darken, and of dark colors to lighten.

These color changes, caused by atmospheric haze, provide an effective means of achieving depth in a visual composition. In Figure 6.4, the successive layers of a building have been rendered in elevation. The red wall of the foreground is drawn as a saturated color, rich and intense in pigment. This same color, seen at a distance, becomes a very weak pink that removes it visually from the front of the picture. It is an effective technique to render the successive layers of a building when it is viewed as a flat elevation.

Space Defined by Color Boundaries

The techniques of the Ecole des Beaux-Arts for rendering shade and shadow were explored in Chapter 4. The construction of shade and shadow is perhaps the most enduring of all the procedures for achieving the illusion of space in architectural drawing. The principles by which these washes were applied in the Beaux-Arts were so clearly articulated that they suggest ways in which the process could be automated on the computer. But although these are useful procedures for studying and presenting buildings, there is something repugnant to most designers about the suggestion of automation. Josef Albers would probably let the eye judge such a situation, for as long as two or more colors interact as the designer would have them interact, then computation has been a useful tool. When these color selections are not to his or her liking, then it is time to intervene.

The essential ingredient of the Beaux-Arts technique for determining shade and shadow is the location of color boundaries. The edge, or boundary, of an object in sunlight was projected onto the object behind it. The shadow was carefully drawn and its edge was rendered with a strong, dark value. The result was a definition of space—objects in sunlight were light in value, objects on which shadows were cast were rendered in a much darker tone.

The question raised by Albers is why colors behave this way. Why do some colors combine to form a surface, while others will move into the background and imply a space between the two colors? In part the answer is to be found in the implications of transparency that several colors in combination can develop, but that is only a partial answer. The rendered shades and shadows of Beaux-Arts drawings effectively suggest space without any apparent implication of transparency.

It is possible to define an object's position in space by its color, or rather by the way its chosen color relates to adjacent colors. This is the secret Albers has revealed, the principle behind the work of the Beaux-Arts. In Figure 6.5, three vertical black bars are shown in relation to a horizontal bar of white. It is a spatial composition in that some objects appear in front of others. The animation of the drawing develops from a spatial reading of the bars; the white bar seems to

FIGURE 6.5.   Transparency. Computer adaptation from a design by Josef Albers 1963. (Graphic: the author)

weave between the three transparent black forms. On the left, a black bar is read as transparent and is located in front of the white bar; on the right-hand side, the white bar is seen to move in front of the black.

Transparency must be carefully regulated in order to control the position of these objects in space. Why, you ask, does the black form on the left appear to be located on top of the white form? Albers would have you look at the lines that form the boundary of each shape (Albers 1963). Focus on the center portion of the left-hand black form in the drawing, just the part that overlaps the white bar. In the computer, this shape is a discrete color. On the top and the bottom of the black form, where the shape is read as continuous, the contrast of value with the adjacent black is minimal—a weak color boundary is established. Compare this to the left and right edges of the rectangle, where a strong value contrast exists between the gray of the form and the adjacent white—here a strong boundary is established.

It is the boundary, the edge of the colored figure, that determines its spatial position. On the left, the black form is made to read on top of the white shape because of the value contrasts established at its boundaries. The weaker boundary conditions tie the form to the adjacent color area: the stronger boundary conditions separate the form from the adjacent color to suggest spatial difference. By composition, and by choice of colors, the black form on the left is located on top of the white bar.

Look now at the right side of this composition, where the white bar has moved to a forward position in the picture. Color choices for the boundaries of the central shape have changed. The top and bottom edges form weak boundaries; the left and right edges are strong. By manipulation of these value contrasts, the position of the bars in space has been changed. While based on the phenomenon of transparency, the central issue is one of determining spatial position.

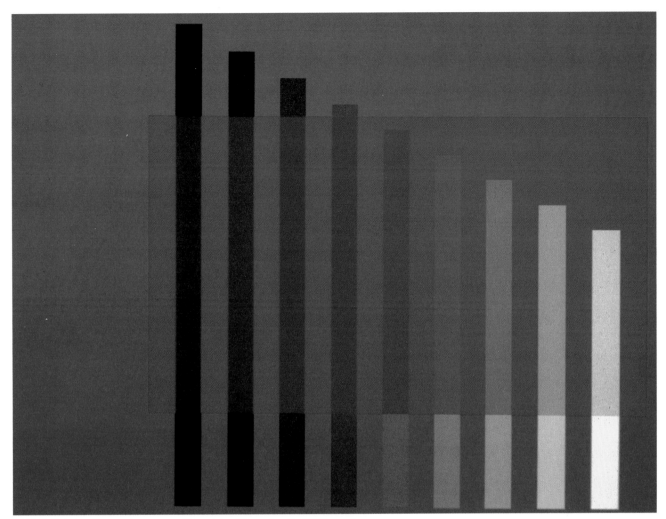

FIGURE 6.6.   Forms in space. (Graphic: Timothy D. Williams)

Using value contrast to locate objects in space is an intriguing concept. Can what is done with contrast of value also be achieved with the other six Itten contrasts? Figure 6.6 is a computer study of the movement of forms in space based on these concepts. Through the manipulation of color boundaries, the forms are given rhythm and movement beyond the two dimensions of the composition.

Architectural forms can be defined spatially by the selection of color for their parts. In Figure 6.7, contrasts of both value and hue are used to define a collection of forms that suggest architecture. Control of a form's color, and control of the adjacent colors that determine the boundary contrast, are essential to the visualization of architectural form on the computer.

Figure 6.8 is a computer drawing based on a study of Josef Albers. It shows a progresssion of nine red bars dancing spatially around a transparent horizontal band of yellow. This is a somewhat difficult composition to render on the computer, for it requires the selection of twelve colors. In this case, the drawing was done on a computer with only a sixty-four-color capability, displaying sixteen at a time; the

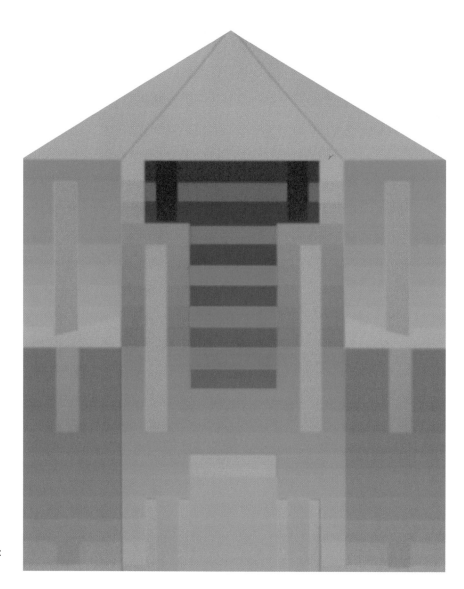

FIGURE 6.7.   Houseform. (Graphic:
David Owen Loy)

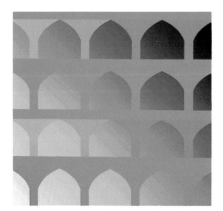

FIGURE 6.8.   Arches. (Graphic:
Clifford D. Kinard III)

limited choices of color account for some of the color variations seen
in the drawing. But by using techniques for mixing the pixels of color
on the screen, a fair copy of the Albers composition was achieved. The
red bars in the illustration appear to be on top of the yellow band at
the left-hand edge of the picture. As the eye moves from left to right,
the bars gradually dissolve into the composition, while the yellow
band emerges on top. An array of transparencies is involved in the
composition in order to make this transition; value contrasts are controlled in order to unite the red forms to the left, the yellow forms to
the right.

An electronic colorist can use most of the techniques of both
painter and renderer, with the added advantage of being able to modify colors selectively until he achieves his objectives. The arcade
shown in Figure 6.9 is a study in color boundaries. A series of green
arches is shown rendered over a changing green background. There
are color changes within the arch forms, but the arcade is made to
stand out as a unit, developing continuity as a continuous form, by

maintaining stronger boundary contrasts with the background colors than within the arcade itself.

This same control of boundaries can be found in the work of the impressionist painters discussed in Chapter 2. While Itten described these spatial manipulations in terms of contrast, Josef Albers referred to the color boundaries within the painting. In Toulouse-Lautrec's *At the Moulin Rouge* (Figure 2.27), areas of activity color within the painting are defined by color boundaries, uniting these as groups and separating them from other areas of the painting. A foreground group, seated at the table, is seen in dark tones that contrast with the figures beyond. The variations of color within this group are rich—the scarlet trim on the color in the foreground, the modeling of the heavy coats. But continuity of shape is maintained because boundary contrasts within the group are never allowed to become as strong as they are with the café scene behind. By arranging the groups with care, the observer is led through the painting, forming a sense of depth in imagination, experiencing the perspective by virtue of the colors that the artist has selected.

The creation of space is an old and important banner of the modern movement. The writings of Le Corbusier, of Sigfried Giedion, of Bruno Zevi—all reinforce design as the process of manipulating form to define space. The possibilities offered by using electronic color to visualize space and the spatial complexities of a design are as significant as the developments in computer perspective. While perspective drawing can indicate the arrangement of architectural space, electronic color promises to give insight into the quality of that space, with the potential for illuminating it with reality, or with illusion, to illustrate and to clarify the concept of a design.

FIGURE 6.9.   Transparency.
Computer adaptation from a design by Josef Albers 1963. (Graphic: G. Scott Kilgore, Sr.)

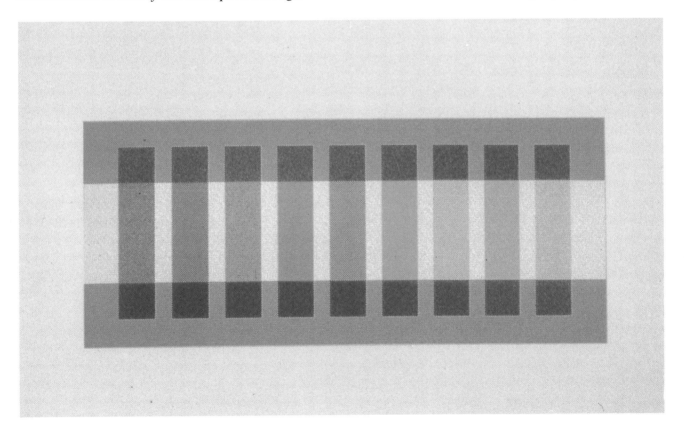

DEFINITION OF FORM

The surface of any building has many rhythms. Some are the result of light that is cast upon the surface, forming shadows that sculpt the building mass. Other rhythms develop from the nature of the surface itself, its textures and changes in plane. The definition of surfaces electronically should reflect this diversity, suggesting appropriate texture where it exists and casting shadows in a realistic way.

Surface Defined by Color Boundaries

Color boundaries can define surface as well as space. Look once more at Figure 6.8. Note that not all parts of the composition imply depth. While the definition of space is clear at the ends of the composition, at some point in this picture the red bars are neither behind nor in front of the yellow band; one of these bars, somewhere in the center of the composition, is deliberately and obviously in the same plane as the yellow band. This point, somewhere near the middle of the composition, occurs when the color boundaries achieve what Albers calls a *middle mix*. At this point the contrast of value at each color edge appears balanced; boundaries at the top and bottom of this red bar contrast equally with those on its left and right sides. In this situation the two forms, the red bars and the yellow band, develop a flat quality. There is a cohesiveness developed by the coloration that unites them in one plane.

A symphony in these gradations was illustrated by Albers in a particularly difficult graphic composition, a computerized adaptation of which is shown in Figure 6.10. It was a difficult graphic to produce, both for Albers and for a student with a sixty-four-color palette on the computer. The production of this graphic involved the careful balance of thirteen color choices, woven as three stripes of color mixed with three bands of yellow. Properly executed, this should illustrate the three elements of foreground, background, and what Albers refers to as the " illusive middle mix" (Albers 1963). The illustration is included here as much for the imperfections necessitated by the use of this primitive computer, as to demonstrate virtuosity of color control. Carefully balanced, color can either emphasize or deny the sensation of depth.

By control of value contrasts at the edge of shapes, it is possible to reinforce the feeling of "surface" in a composition, to enhance the surface quality of a form. Figure 6.11 shows a simple progression of blues. There is nothing in these colors to suggest that one form is in front of another; they appear to be on the same plane. This is partially due to composition. They are arranged in a line, and the scalloping of the edge helps to unite the composition. More important, the color boundary between each band is equally strong; the value contrast is expressed in equal steps.

This equal progression of colors is what was referred to in Chapter 5 as a color ramp. As long as each step in the ramp is uniform, there is no sense of space; on the contrary, the elements seem glued, one to another, in an inseparable pattern. Their connection can be explained in terms of simultaneous contrast (see Chapter 2). Let's try a slow-motion experiment. As your eye moves from one edge of a color area

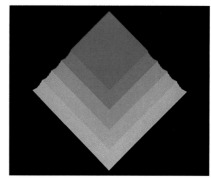

FIGURE 6.11. Transparency. Computer adaptation from a design by Josef Albers 1963. (Graphic: Peter R. Wehner)

FIGURE 6.10. Space illusion. Computer adaptation from a design by Josef Albers 1963. (Graphic: the author)

toward another, it has been fatigued by the color just seen; that color is removed from the visual experience. Each band of color is robbed at its boundary by the adjacent color. The result is an unevenness, even though each color sample is totally flat and consistent. The unevenness is an optical illusion; it can be perceived as an error in the coloring of the surface. But as a technique, the adjacent colors bond to express a unit of surface.

Architectural Massing

The unevenness within each color sample produced by a color ramp can be used to advantage, for it is a method of giving depth to a totally flat panel of color. An architectural surface offers the designer a rich opportunity to display sensitivity to form. Walls are not flat planes of color. By the selection of surface treatment, a designer is able to give scale to building, to modify the proportions of the design, or to provide clues that will relate the form of the building to its context. Figure 6.12 is a computer rendering of a house designed by the well-known architect, Helmut Jahn. The form of the building is rendered as far more than a simple kindergarten block; its surfaces are developed with line and with color to articulate and enhance the simple geometric form. There is no stonework in this articulation, no brick pattern or heavy material to give texture. The form is created with color.

A building can be textured with color just as it can be with stone —the color becomes almost a surrogate texture. The color effects are neither accidental nor capricious if they are developed with a good understanding of color boundaries and the way they affect the perception of adjacent colors. The colors of the panels that form the façade

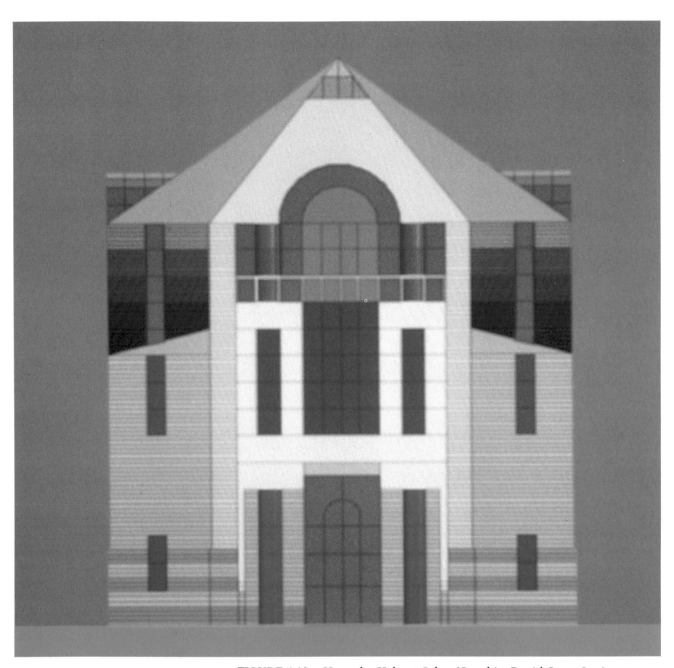

FIGURE 6.12.   House by Helmut Jahn. (Graphic: David Owen Loy)

of I. M. Pei's addition to the Museum of Modern Art in New York City are selected in a progression that enlivens the surface and provides a texture.

Figure 6.13 is a simplified rendering of the massing of I. M. Pei's National Center for Atmospheric Research in Boulder, Colorado. The scale of the building is massive, no doubt the intent of the architect. In Figure 6.14 the building has been reproportioned not by changing the massing, but by changing the color to reduce the appearance of mass. These changes in color strongly affect the building's form, giving it a more diminutive scale. The computer makes such options simple.

In the design studio, consideration of surface color can be a pow-

FIGURE 6.13.   National Center for Atmospheric Research, Boulder,
Colorado. I. M. Pei, Architect. (Graphic: Mark Sangiolo)

FIGURE 6.14.   Research Center modified. (Graphic: Mark Sangiolo)

FIGURE 6.15.   Timbuktoo design competition entry. (Graphic: Renee M. D'Adamo)

erful tool in shaping buildings. The structure shown in Figure 6.15, for example, was designed for a desert environment. The harshness of the architectural form was softened by using an undulating color scheme but the building still appeared too massive for the environment. An alternative, shown in Figure 6.16, reduces the mass and blends it with the colors of the desert.

Today, more than at any other time, the surfaces of structures can be formed with colored elements. To the metal curtain walls of the modern movement have been added the colored stucco surfaces and synthetic materials of all sorts; a rainbow of paint is available to treat virtually any material. Historically, architecture has at times been very involved with color. Figure 6.17 uses the color capabilities of the computer to attempt a reconstruction of the colors believed to be used by the ancient Greeks on the Parthenon. Figure 6.18 uses color to a different purpose on another historic building by attempting to articulate the massing of the Pantheon in Rome through the use of hue changes alone; by the selection of different hues of red, it is possible to suggest the rounded form of the dome. In Figure 6.19 this massing changes, emphasizing the element over the front of the building. These studies are crude in a color sense, and based on a very minimal color capability; they do, however, illustrate how even rudimentary color capacities can be manipulated to convey spatial messages.

A well-known architect once told the story of standing on a hilltop

FIGURE 6.16.   Timbuktoo design competition entry. (Graphic: Renee M. D'Adamo)

FIGURE 6.17.   The Parthenon. (Graphic: Todd Boggess)

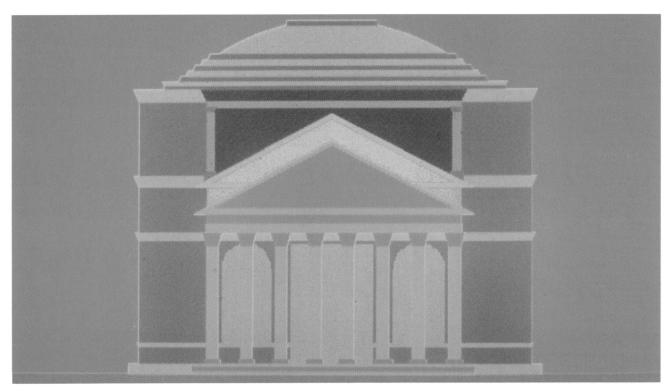

FIGURE 6.18.   Color study of the Pantheon. (Graphic: William J. Blackmon)

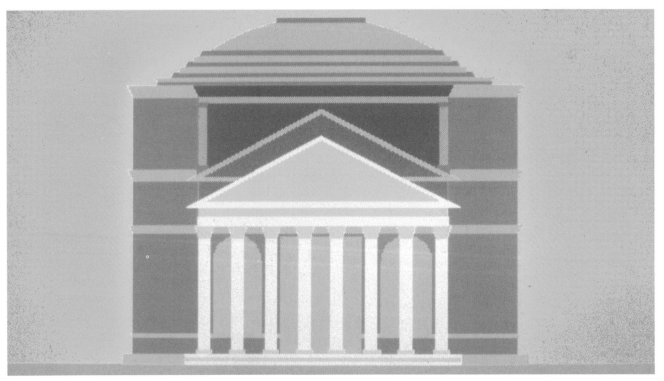

FIGURE 6.19.   Color study of the Pantheon. (Graphic: William J. Blackmon)

overlooking one of America's growing cities, and observing its larger "monuments" to the modern movement. "The buildings are available in black, white, and gray," he said, gesturing to the cityscape; "They can be horizontal, vertical, or neutral." Color is what makes a building horizontal, vertical, or neutral. In Figures 6.20 and 6.21, two views of the same building are seen; only the colors of the elements have changed. By adjusting the color boundaries, a vertical continuity is assured in one case, and a horizontal continuity in the other. In the knowing hand of a designer, color can be a powerful tool; by changing the color of a structure, its proportion is changed. The towers shown in Figures 6.22 and 6.23 achieve the same changes on a larger, though

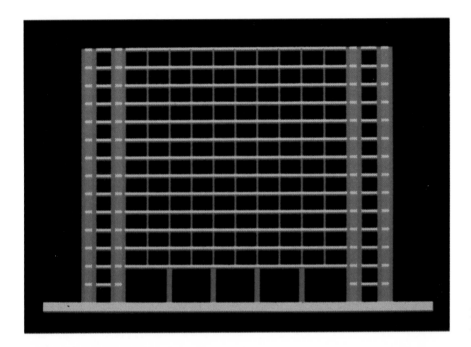

FIGURE 6.20.   Horizontal massing study. (Graphic: Sharon D. Eleazer)

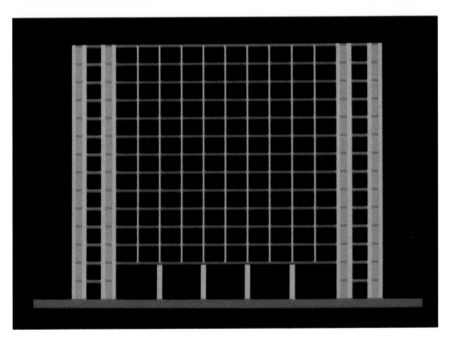

FIGURE 6.21.   Vertical massing study. (Graphic: Sharon D. Eleazer)

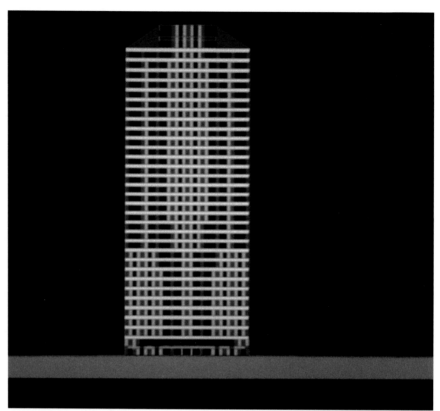

FIGURE 6.22.   Horizontal massing study for a tower. (Graphic: David Reilly)

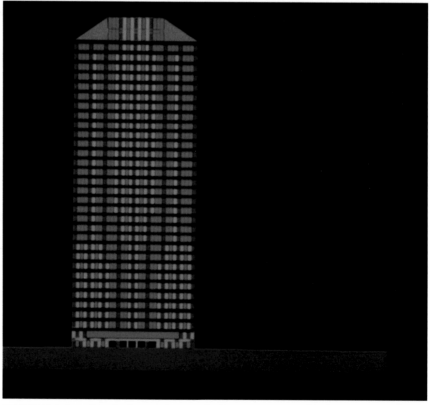

FIGURE 6.23.   Vertical massing study for a tower. (Graphic: David Reilly)

perhaps more subtle scale.

The surfaces of buildings are but paintboards awaiting the choices of a sensitive designer to specify colors that will bring the mass to life, fit it properly into its environment, relate it to its context, and give it a scale with which people can feel comfortable. The selection of these colors is rightly a part of the process of designing a building, and computers make this possible. The secrets of color behavior that control this design work are not new; many of them can be found in the work of Josef Albers (Albers 1963).

EXERCISES

1. Define an abstract landscape or architectural scene as a series of planes in which atmospheric illusion is used to give depth to the composition. Prove the validity of your solution by demonstrating alternatives. How do changes of value or of saturation affect the composition?
2. Develop a composition that explains color boundaries by locating objects both in front of and behind a plane. Does your drawing illustrate the concept of the middle mix?
3. Choose a simple architectural elevation and explore alternative massing of the elements by changing the colors of the drawing.

REFERENCES

Albers, Josef. 1963. *Interaction of Color.* New Haven, CT: Yale University Press.

Munsell, Albert. 1976 [1924]. *The Munsell Book of Color.* Baltimore: Munsell Color Company, Inc.

Weber, Nicholas Fox. 1988. The artist as alchemist. In *Joseph Albers: A Retrospective.* New York: Solomon R. Guggenheim Museum.

Chapter 7

Color Psychology

Color can be a joy to experience. Who has not awakened in the yellow light of morning as the sun bathes the world in glorious color? Color stirs the soul and fires the imagination. People react to color; they are made happy by the green of the trees, by a field of yellow flowers, or by the color of grass rippling in a summer breeze. Tiring of the pallor of winter colors, we take long trips to experience the bloom of azaleas in the springtime of a southern garden; in the fall we make pilgrimages to see the changing colors of autumn leaves.

But the appeal of color is not limited to nature. The whitewashed villages of the Greek islands are appealing under a blue Mediterranean sky, as are the umber tones of the Italian hill towns. The harmony that is caused by well-chosen color has an undeniable appeal. When cities are colored in a uniform way, as with the traditional stone façades of Paris, this uniformity attracts us and arouses our sense of order. Today the color control that comes with a limited palette of building materials has all but disappeared, a victim of the prolific material choices that confront designers. On an urban scale, it is exceedingly difficult to find examples of appealing, appropriate color selection.

On a smaller scale, examples of meaningful color are easier to find. The architecture of Luis Barragan has long been known for its successful coloration; the recent color statements of I. M. Pei, Cesar Pelli, and Antoine Predock, to name a few, have been successful with individual buildings. But more often the interior of a building provides an opportunity for the control of all aspects of the color environment. Examples abound of rooms that excite, inspire, calm, or even disturb people. When the total coloration of an environment can be controlled, a designer is able to use color to shape places in a more meaningful way.

The experience of colors and the sensations they can evoke in the mind are real; and to a large degree, they are predictable. They can develop from experience, like reactions to the colors of a flag or a uniform. This is a very culture-dependent phenomenon; we would not expect a Japanese to react to the display of red, white, and blue with the same feeling of patriotism as an American or a Frenchman. Likewise, the association of white with weddings, while typical in American culture, is not a universal phenomenon; it is unknown in the

Orient. Often color reactions are learned by association. Foods are a good example of this. We expect our meat to be red and our salads green; our taste buds have conditioned us to this and we reject variations from the norm—a plate of green potatoes or blue meat is never popular fare.

When you plan a building, there are times when a particular material choice may be a better selection because of its color. It is too often stated, in selecting colors, that "beauty is in the eye of the beholder." Sometimes red, or any particular hue, is in fact the "best" color choice, because individuals usually react to that color in a manner that fulfills the designer's intent for the space.

Armed with a knowledge of how people react to a particular color, we can make color selections that will temper a person's reaction to the design; the electronic colorist can use color knowledge to produce spaces that create joy, solemnity, or fear—color then reinforces the intent of the design. In selecting colors, the first decision is usually an empirical determination of a dominant hue. This choice can be made on the basis of taste alone, though more logically it should be supported with some knowledge of color psychology. As a designer, you can explore color choices on the computer and react to your knowledge of how color affects people. Through the application of psychology, you will discover why one hue may be better than another for a given situation. Through computation, the logic that is a part of the design process can be extended to the selection of color.

THE MEANING OF COLOR

Humans have long sought to give meaning to color. Ancient Egyptians used colors whose symbolic connotations evolved in prehistory—color was a part of the hieroglyphic message. The stone temples of ancient Greece were not left a natural color, but richly painted in colors founded on both tradition and symbolism. Leonardo da Vinci equated colors to the ancient elements—he designated yellow as earth, red as fire, green as water, and blue as air (Verity 1980, 115).

The physics of color is now well understood. The physiology of the eye and the mechanics of how the human brain receives color information have been well documented. In the arts too, color models provide an explanation of color relationships. But the psychology of color, that reaction experienced by individuals to particular colorations, is neither clearly defined nor often used in architectural design. The rationale of design frequently stops short of color selection—we turn instead to tradition and prejudice. There are color principles, predictable experiences from reactions to particular colors. With the new color tools available, logical color selections can be made that will enhance the concept of a design.

Johann Wolfgang von Goethe

Modern color psychology began with the work of the German poet and dramatist Johann Wolfgang von Goethe (1747–1832). Goethe's color model is discussed in Chapter 3. His was a challenge to the physical system proposed by Newton. To Goethe, it was more essential to comprehend the human reaction to a color than to understand its physics. The color model he proposed is based on a human reaction to color, rather than the physical cause of color sensation.

His color theory, given its philosophical base, is more subject to interpretation than are scientific theories. The proof is more difficult. In 1808, Goethe wrote:

> The coloring of most modern painters is without character, for, while they follow their general instinctive feeling only, the last result of such a tendency must be mere completeness; this, they more or less attain, but . . . at the same time neglect the characteristic impression which the subject might demand. (Matthaei 1971, 185)

Goethe's theory of color is monumental in the evolution of contemporary color ideas. Its uniqueness can be explained by his concern for the meaning of color. This is not a scientific investigation, for Goethe would more often record what he felt a color to be saying than what he had learned from observation. Writing as he did in the early part of the industrial revolution, his humanistic outcry was a welcome counterpoint to a period dominated by scientific discovery.

> Since I cannot present irrefutable evidence, which would have to be based upon complete experience, I only ask that you might expose my thoughts to your own consciousness in order to understand what I mean. Namely, that a painter does not deal with any other elements than the one you will find here. (Matthaei 1971, 191)

What Goethe presents is a psychological color ordering rather than a system of classification—each color is equated to the particular emotions its use in painting will evoke. We know that the reaction to color is more emotional than rational; yet these reactions are so tempered by tradition and experience that they become difficult to predict.

The psychological reactions to colors are carefully systematized by Goethe. His model becomes as much a metaphor of human emotion as it is a model of color relationships. His descriptions have developed an enduring quality despite their "conscious" origins. The ideas Goethe proposed in his theory of color were a source of inspiration for the artists of the Bauhaus—both Itten and Albers acknowledge his ideas and interpret them heavily in the development of their own philosophies and attitudes.

Goethe's color circle is divided into six equal divisions of color. The colors, red, orange, yellow, green, blue, and violet, are his own lists. While correctly drawn in a circle, their psychological ordering can best be expressed in the equilateral triangle shown in Figure 7.1. This is an abstraction of the original color tetrahedron developed by Goethe (Matthaei 1971, 188). It appears and is expanded by Joseph Albers in his own description of color theories and color systems (Albers, 1963, 66). It is further explored as a source of color logic by Uwe Koos in developing harmonious color systems (Koos 1982, 12).

In Goethe's words: "Experience teaches us that particular colors excite particular states of feeling" (Matthaei, 1971, 168). In the color triangle the primary colors are indicated at the corners: red, yellow, and blue. This list is Goethe's invention; he equates the colors emotionally to factors affecting the human senses. Red is representative of

FIGURE 7.1.   The harmonic triangle, attributed to Goethe. (Graphic: the author)

imagination, the inventive quality in us; yellow is equated to *reason*, the unique ability of the human mind; blue represents *understanding*, the assimilation of accumulated knowledge. From this trilogy of human sensuality, their mixture and combination, Goethe is able to account for all the factors of human emotional experience.

The combination of these sensibilities can also be expressed in color. The primary hues are combined to form three further colors: orange, violet, and green. These secondary colors Goethe has located between the primary colors on his color circle. They represent further emotions—derivative of the first, combined as the mind would combine them. Such descriptions can quickly become prescriptions for artists mixing paint, and in fact many color theories have been derived to provide this guidance (Koos 1982, 13). But the model Goethe devised serves allegorically as a model of the human mind. In this simple triangle, and the combinations of color that it implies, can be found the entire gamut of human emotions.

Wassily Kandinsky

Of all the artists at the Bauhaus it was particularly Wassily Kandinsky (1866–1944) who took up the banner of Goethean color psychology and brought it into twentieth century. Kandinsky could be called the father of abstract art; he had established himself as both an abstract painter and an author when he was asked to become a Master of Form at the Bauhaus by Walter Gropius in 1921 (Whitford 1984, 95).

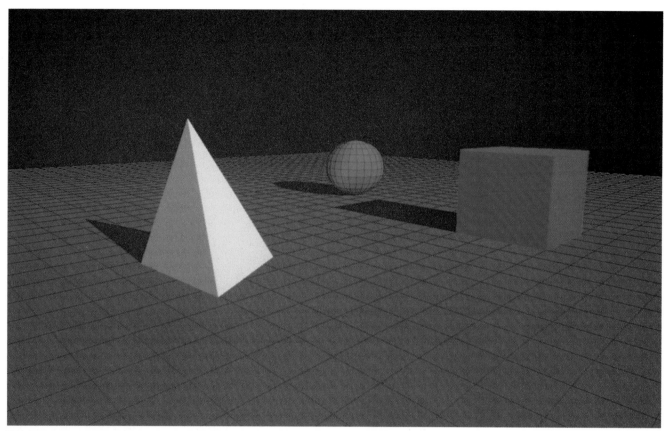

FIGURE 7.2.   Spatial composition of basic forms and colors. (Graphic:
John M. Young, Jr.)

Kandinsky's ideas on the arts were consistent with Bauhaus
thinking; he was a link with the more romantic figures of the German
tradition, largely through Goethe. Kandinsky believed in the concept
of *Gesamtkunstwerk*, the unity of the arts, a romantic tradition advocated by Richard Wagner in his operas.

Some of the more peculiar "dictates" of the Bauhaus were their
collective beliefs on the relationship of color to form. The origins of
these beliefs could probably be credited to Kandinsky—his search for
relationships between painting and art led him to equate basic forms
with basic colors. Kandinsky felt that the brittle, outward-reaching
nature of yellow was most compatible with the angular form of the
triangle. On the other hand blue, being a firm and receding color, was
best represented with the circle. Red, central to his system of color,
was represented with the square. In this simplistic manner, the three
basic geometric shapes were each given a color identity (Figure 7.2).
The extension of this to cube, sphere, and tetrahedron was but a logical step that enabled the Bauhaus faculty to relate color to both sculpture and architectural form (Poling 1986, 72). It is probably fortunate
that Kandinsky's teachings have not prevailed in this respect, for a
dictate to render architectural elements with this formula would, in
retrospect, not have improved the outward appearance of the modern
movement in architecture. (It might be noted in passing that the modern preference for rectilinear form would, according to Goethe, indicate a prevalance of imagination over reason or understanding.)

Nevertheless, an affinity between form and color must be conceded. This fundamental color-form relationship became a thematic image of the Bauhaus—it was adopted in ballet, in architecture, and in painting. It has become the single most memorable image of the Bauhaus era.

Kandinsky preferred to picture the relationship between colors on a linear scale, rather than as a circle of color. Yellow he visualized as developing out of white and strongly related to it; blue was a progression from black (Poling 1986, 59). All the hues could be arranged in a linear fashion from yellow through red to blue in a way not unlike that of Aguilonius in the seventeenth century. They could also be arranged in the other direction through green rather than red, Kandinsky felt, for while yellow and blue were polar, red and green were spatially interchangeable (Figure 7.3).

As an active painter and a teacher of painting, Kandinsky was searching for a universal system of color, a psychological ordering that would provide a logical basis for color choices. His arrangement made use of three important colors—yellow and blue at the poles, and red as the central and dominating hue. This triad has endured and dominated the teaching of color theory in American art schools; the designation of red, yellow, and blue as primary colors is widely accepted, though it is based more on the Kandinsky/Goethe notions of color psychology than it is on the physical nature of color.

All colors were approached by Kandinsky as pairs; yellow and blue were the poles of a color system dominated by what he con-

FIGURE 7.3.   Kandinsky's linear concept of color. (Graphic: the author)

sidered the two great color divisions: warm and cool. He based a color psychology on this duality, drawing from the active, advancing nature of yellow in half of the spectrum, and the passive, retreating nature of blue in the other half. Kandinsky adhered strongly to the beliefs of Goethe in the material he presented at the Bauhaus. The list of colors he developed and the emotions that he would attribute to them were virtually indistinguishable from those defined earlier by Goethe (Poling 1986, 46).

Both Goethe and Kandinsky expressed the nature of color as pairs of opposing ideas. Itten would call these complementary contrasts; both colors and ideas that are in opposition. In equal balance, they neutralize each other.

THE COLORS

The six colors of the modern computer can be found in the teaching of Kandinsky or Goethe, though their spacing has changed and therefore their complements are redefined. They are presented here as pairs of color, along with a summation of the human response they evoke. It should be emphasized that these are not the primary colors of Kandinsky nor of Goethe, but rather the physical list of colors developed from modern physics.

The responses listed are taken from Goethe, from Albers, and from Kandinsky, in order to summarize the feelings that are known or supposed about each color. Although it is easy to make these generalities about the hues involved, it is more difficult to predict what each value and each saturation of a color will yield as a human response; this, for the colorist, requires a lifetime of experience and experiment. As for the electronic colorist, the colors are easily found; their effective and forceful use, however, will not come from the computer, but from the colorist.

Red

Red is an additive primary color (Figure 7.4), the complement of cyan. It is one of the three light sources in a color computer monitor. Of the three basic reactions to color described by Goethe, red is suggestive of *imagination*. It evokes a festive mood. In the Bauhaus analogy of color and form, red is the color equivalent of the square and its spatial extension, the cube.

According to Goethe, red is the color of heroes; it is sanguine, made of the blood spilled in war. Physically it is a transitional color between the sensations of warm and cool; red hues may be selected to imply either characteristic.

Red is a festive color, capable of great brilliance and so more often employed as an accent than as an overall coloration. When it is used architecturally it can form a space of great dignity and gravity, as in the chamber of a Renaissance palace that has been papered in red, or in a contemporary auditorium where red becomes by choice the dominant hue.

But red is also the mother color of the earth tones, those colors that we associate with the earth; raw umber and burnt sienna are

FIGURE 7.4.   Red.

FIGURE 7.5.   Cyan.

FIGURE 7.6.   Green.

FIGURE 7.7.   Magenta.

shades of red in a low value and with a reduced saturation. The color of wood ranges from red to yellow, in a very low saturation. Frank Lloyd Wright selected Cherokee red as his signature and color of preference.

Cyan

Cyan is a subtractive primary color (Figure 7.5), the complement of red. It is one of the four inks used in color printing. The blue that is discussed by Kandinsky, the blue often spoken of as a "primary or process blue," is similar to cyan, though neither as light or as green.

Cyan is the color of the sky; more properly it is greener than the sky and bluer than the sea. While not as light as sunlight, Gerritsen would classify it as the second lightest of the primary colors at full saturation. Like red, cyan is on the edge of coolness and warmth, and can move a color scheme in either direction.

Cyan is a quiet color. Goethe finds it appropriate to orators, and calls it a phlegmatic color—cold and yet possessed of a calm fortitude. There is a great deal of the contemplative implied in the use of cyan.

Green

Green is an additive primary color (Figure 7.6), the complement of magenta. It has not traditionally been considered a primary color. Green is one of the three light sources in a color computer monitor, and the most intense color the computer screen is capable of providing —the phosphors used produce an intensity of green hue for which there is no precedent. These colors provide a considerable expansion of the Munsell scale.

Kandinsky suggests that green may be substituted for red; like red, it is between the warm and cool colors and capable of each emotion. The colors of the forest are often alive with this warm–cool sensation, as the yellow-green of the poplar is contrasted with the blue-green of the pine; the same contrast exists as the leaves are seen alternately in sunlight and in shade.

Goethe refers to green as the color of poets, described as the easiest of colors to live with constantly. Nature seems to provide ample opportunity for this. The Bauhaus teachers assigned no form to green, preferring to leave it as a natural hue that did not become a forceful part of their color vocabulary.

Magenta

Magenta is a subtractive primary color (Figure 7.7), the complement of green. It is one of the four inks used in color printing.

Magenta is not a natural color; that is to say, it does not occur in the spectrum of light projected from a prism. On the CIE chromaticity chart discussed in Chapter 4, magenta occurs along the flat side of the figure—the Newtonian connection between red and blue. It does appear in nature each spring as the azaleas bloom; in them, there is nothing artificial about magenta.

Kandinsky would define magenta as a color lying on the cool side of red. Goethe calls it a melancholic color, the color of monarchs. It is a cool color, purple in its darker shades and scarlet when light in value —colors that by association are tied to royalty and to the vestments of the Christian church.

Blue

Blue is an additive primary color (Figure 7.8), the complement of yellow. It is one of the three light sources in a color computer monitor. Of the three basic reactions to color described by Goethe, blue is suggestive of *understanding*. It evokes a quiet mood. In the Bauhaus analogy of color and form, blue is the color equivalent of the circle and its spatial extension, the sphere.

FIGURE 7.8. Blue.

The complementary pair of yellow and blue are to Kandinsky the key to the colors. He titled this contrast the most important polar opposition, for they are at the threshold of light on the one hand and darkness on the other. They are the most extreme of the complements. Blue is a powerful, deep, cool color; probably cooler and deeper in its computer interpretation as an ultramarine blue than even the sky-blue of Goethe's color circle.

Goethe pictures blue as capable of expanding space, making it appear larger than it is, though it also presents space as cool and in the shadows (Matthaei 1971, 170). This is consistent with Kandinsky, who describes blue as having a centripetal effect that removes it from the viewer (Poling 1986, 51).

Yellow

Yellow is a subtractive primary color (Figure 7.9), the complement of blue. It is one of the four inks used in color printing. Of the three basic reactions to color described by Goethe, yellow is suggestive of *reason*. It evokes a happy mood. In the Bauhaus analogy of color and form, yellow is the color equivalent of the triangle and its spatial extension, the tetrahedron.

FIGURE 7.9. Yellow.

Yellow, according to Goethe, is the color of *bonvivants*, a color shared by adventurers and lovers. It is the color of gold, symbolic of wealth and power. It is also the color of "common cloth," material too poor to be dyed; yellow can suggest both the good and the bad; Goethe classifies its temperament as "choleric" (hot-tempered), yet capable of being both magnificent and noble when properly used.

This is the color that according to Kandinsky develops from white; it is, like the light of the sun, an exhilarating color, both active and aggressive. It evokes all the excitement, the gaiety and exuberance evoked by the warmth of the sun.

It is yellow that provides the warmth and joy of performance that Louis Sullivan achieved in the design of his Auditorium theater, where the glow of a thousand tungsten filament lights was first experienced in a major public space, reflecting in the gold-foil arches overhead.

The dominant character of yellow is its inherent lightness; it is the color closest to sunlight. It is a happy, gay color, and its use suggests a happy mood. It is, as Kandinsky points out, an intense mood, hard and vibrating.

COLOR TRANSPOSITION

Among the various color manipulations that have been demonstrated by Josef Albers is a discussion of color transposition (Albers 1963, 34). One can draw a logical analogy between musical notes and the colors. Transpositions are common in music; melodies are easily moved from one key to another and every musician has the opportunity to hear music in the various keys to determine how it is most appropriately played. A familiar song is identifiable, regardless of the key signature, and the same could be said of a color composition.

Transposition in color is generally considered to be a change from one hue to another. Value and saturation transpositions are also possible—a film negative is essentially a value transposition. But value transpositions are not translations, as occur in music, to another presentable form; their use is more technical. Transposition of hue is often a useful technique in considering alternative color choices.

In exploring psychological color change, it is often desirable to change the colors of a building or of a composition and to see the outcome of the selection. One could, of course, decide a color usage in advance—decide, for example, that yellow was an appropriate dominant color choice for the design; but such decisions are usually based on personal taste or preconception, rather than on a conscious decision to manipulate reactions.

If color psychology is be used well, the sensitive designer would want to balance the visual appearance of the design with the psychological effects that can be predicted from the color choices. Traditionally, this was not easy. In selecting colors for a building, it is an exhaustive chore to acquire samples of all the materials and colors involved; one is seldom driven to doing this twice. A more sensitive color selection could be made if the outcome of two sets of decisions could be seen, especially if those decisions were based not only on what one sees, but also on what one knows about the colors involved and how they will affect the experience of the intended users.

Figure 7.10 is a computerized version of a graphic by Josef Albers. Because of the composition the eye will read the diagonal rectangle as one figure, even though the left and right portions appear to be different colors. With the central color bands removed (Figure 7.11), both halves are shown to be one color. This is a simple but lucid demonstration of how one color can appear to be two different colors.

The advantage to having this composition on a computer is quickly seen; in Figures 7.12 and 7.13 all the hues in the composition have been completely altered. In Figure 7.12 the rectangle has become yellow, and proportionate adjustments have been made to each component color. Figure 7.13 renders the composition in cyan, with similar adjustments in the other colors. These compositions have been processed quickly, making use of the computer to display totally new hue selections. Such transpositions are possible because of the technology of the computer. The task of developing alternative color selections, never easy, becomes feasible on the computer because color information can be separated from compositional information. As in music, there is a key in which the intent of every architectural space is maximized, so there must be a coloration appropriate to every graphic composition. By seeing these choices displayed on the computer screen, the designer can make a better decision.

FIGURE 7.10.   Composition. Computer adaptation from Albers 1963.
(Graphic: the author)

FIGURE 7.11.   Composition modified. Computer adaptation from Albers
1963. (Graphic: the author)

FIGURE 7.12.   Composition transposed to yellow. (Graphic: the author)

FIGURE 7.13.   Composition transposed to cyan. (Graphic: the author)

APPLIED PSYCHOLOGY

Through the use of color transpositions, psychology can become an ally in both the design and the presentation of architecture. Figure 7.14 is a computer composition, an exterior perspective of a house designed by the architect Michael Graves. The color choices in this illustration are those of the graphic designer and represent his own interpretation of which colors would be selected by the architect.

Once a data base of design information for a house is established in the computer, it exists and can be used in many ways to develop appropriate design information. Using the data, the architect is free to explore the effects of color choices in order to anticipate how clients will react. Just as the Albers composition in Figure 7.10 was transposed, so the computerized image of the house can be altered in a variety of ways.

In Figure 7.15 the color selections for the house have been reinterpreted, assuming colors selected by another architect, and with a different design intent. (Some architects have exhibited such strong color preferences that their work can be distinguished by its color). Changes

FIGURE 7.14.   Computer rendering of the Plocek House by Michael Graves.
(Graphic: David Owen Loy)

FIGURE 7.15.   Transposition of the Plocek House, artist's interpretation of coloration by another architect. (Graphic: David Owen Loy)

of color palette become simple when graphic data are separated from color data. The purpose of this exercise is not to compare architects, but to search for the character of an individual designer as it is expressed through color choice, and to experience the emotional difference between the two colorations. The exercise can be carried even further, using the established data base to explore historical precedent. In Figure 7.16 the house has been further transposed, this time in the guise of a de Stijl architect and reminiscent of the Bauhaus era. Color choices are as much tempered by current fashion as they are by personality.

Character is strongly tied to the selection of colors; consider Figure 7.17, a student's interpretation of Marc Chagall's *Self-portrait*, again drawn on the computer. In an effort to demonstrate the effect of Chagall's color choices on his audience, the colors are then *transposed* to a color palette selected from the work of Frank Lloyd Wright (Figure 7.18). As preposterous as such changes are, they demonstrate the extent to which color selection is an integral part of design.

Occasionally the selection of color is dramatically tempered by experience. Consider, for example, Figure 7.19, the graphic designer's interpretation of colors for a swimming pool area located inside the house previously illustrated, with colors appropriate to the architect.

Once these data are accumulated, the color transpositions considered for the exterior of the house can be applied to the interior. Figure 7.20 indicates the color decisions that might have been made by another architect; Figure 7.21 shows the house with colors characteristic of the de Stijl period. The one constant, through all these transpositions, has been the color of the water in the pool. In each case, the water is drawn as blue. We are conditioned through experience to expect water to be blue, and the graphic designer has carefully selected colors in response to this expectation, using the methods for showing successive depths of transparency demonstrated by Albers (see Chapter 6).

The pool has an inviting, welcome feel to it. One further transposition, however, is studied using the swimming pool data base. In Figure 7.22 the water in the pool has been changed from blue to red. Suddenly there is a feeling of revulsion. Goethe had said that red is sanguine, the color of blood, and the suggestion of blood is strong in this liquid bath of red. No one would want to swim in this pool. Blue is described as cool and calm, just what is expected in a pool, and the designer has responded to the traditions, experiences, and expectations of his audience. Psychology is always with us; to be aware of it and to cultivate its use advantageously in the selection of color can only reinforce the quality of good design.

FIGURE 7.16.   Transposition of the Plocek House, de Stijl coloration. (Graphic: David Owen Loy)

FIGURE 7.17.   Computer adaptation of Marc Chagall's *Self-portrait*. (Graphic: Norman E. Bello, Jr.)

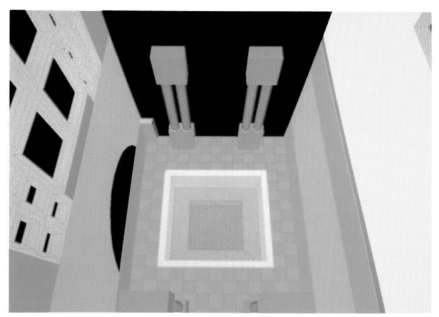

FIGURE 7.19.   Computer adaptation of an interior of the Plocek House by Michael Graves. (Graphic: David Owen Loy)

FIGURE 7.18.   Transposition of Marc Chagall's *Self-portrait*. (Graphic: Norman E. Bello, Jr.)

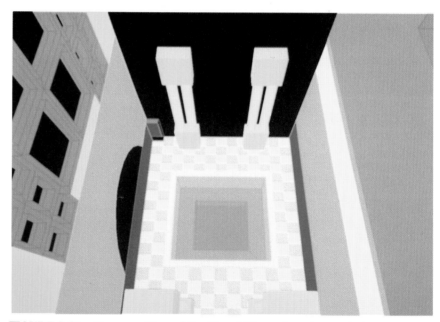

FIGURE 7.20.   Transposition of the Plocek House interior, artist's interpretation of coloration by another architect. (Graphic: David Owen Loy)

FIGURE 7.21.   Transposition of the Plocek House interior, de Stijl coloration. (Graphic: David Owen Loy)

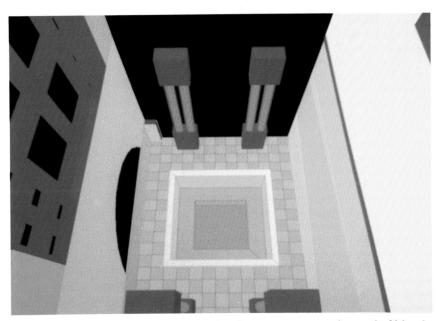

FIGURE 7.22.   Transposition of the Plocek House interior, the pool of blood. (Graphic: David Owen Loy)

EXERCISES

1. Develop an appropriate coloration for a building on the computer screen. Next, modify the color data for that drawing, and suggest how a list of other designers might approach the problem.
2. List the emotions that might be appropriate to a particular architectural place. Next, modify the color base to your rendering of that place, and develop appropriate coloration that suggests these emotions.

REFERENCES

Albers, Josef. 1963. *Interaction of Color.* New Haven, CT: Yale University Press.

Koos, Uwe. 1982. *Basic Introduction to Color Design.* STO AG Stuhlingen, W. Germany: STO-Design Studio (Color Area Space), STO Systems Technology Organization.

Matthaei, Rupprecht, ed. 1971. *Goethe's Color Theory.* American ed. New York: Van Nostrand Reinhold.

Poling, Clark V. 1986. *Kandinsky's Teaching at the Bauhaus: Color Theory and Analytical Drawing.* New York: Rizzoli International Publications.

Verity, Enid. 1980. *Color Observed.* New York: Van Nostrand Reinhold.

Whitford, Frank. 1984. *Bauhaus.* London: Thames and Hudson.

Chapter 8

Color in the Design Process

There is a tradition of good color usage in the design of advertisements and billboards. The posters of Toulouse-Lautrec in the nineteenth century were conceived with color as integral to their message, a practice that continues in modern advertising. Meaningful color usage is expected as a part of graphic art today.

Architects, on the other hand, usually design in black and white; in architecture there is no color tradition that is a part of the design process. This may be partly due to the tools that are used. But architects seem to live between two worlds—the colorful "real" world that is experienced when you put on boots and walk through the countryside or the city streets, and the black and white "studio" world with its collection of drawing pens and papers. Studio design is necessarily concerned with the images of buildings. These are a representation of the other world—an abstraction of what is "out there," or of what you propose to put "out there." Despite the large collection of colored pencils and bottled colors that have become a part of most architectural studios, most abstractions of buildings are drawn with lines, rather than color. As line drawings, they are colorless.

Unlike the graphic designer, architects do not work with their art, but with a representation of their art. You cannot stand on the hillside, like an orchestra leader waving some giant baton, and create buildings. The architect is forced into a world of abstract representation, producing line drawings that speak more often to architects and to the construction industry than to the rest of the population. They require considerable intellectual capacity, coupled with an awareness of visual techniques, in order to be understood. Why would anyone want to cut a building in half, to spend hours drawing what it would look like in a dismembered state? An architect's abstractions often bear little resemblance to what is seen when you enter the "other world."

Electronic media can cause design work to resemble what is out there far more than has been possible with traditional drawing tools.

The architect using a computer to draw is still *representing* the world, though it may become less obvious as the representations begin to look like real objects. There is an advantage in this, for it can remove some of the guesswork from design; you can see what is happening, rather than relying on intuition and judgment; what you see is what you get. There is an advantage too for clients, teachers, or patrons. They do not need to learn the abstract drawing language of the architect. Without any knowledge of visual techniques, they can relate to the design; they can understand the intention of a design and the logic of the designer.

There are also disadvantages to making objects look real. The napkin sketch, those first thoughts for the arrangement of a building that are sometimes drawn on a paper napkin over lunch, can fire the imagination and kindle thoughts that would be killed by a more complete representation, in a situation where the details are simply not known. But the reaction between two colors is not an issue of detail— color can be applied; to the napkin sketch as well as to the finished drawing. Color communicates design ideas as images in real world terms, with a directness that is simply not achieved with traditional line work. A circular area on a drawing could be labeled "lake," or it could be labeled "grass"; without the label, no one knows which is intended. But color the area green or blue, and the intent becomes instantly clear.

THE DISCOVERY OF SITE

The design of any building is first of all a response to its site. Computer imagery can help to visualize this; a simple blue sky background on a computer screen provides a more realistic place to draw a building elevation than does the yellow of a sheet of tracing paper. It places the building against a sky color as it will usually be seen. Through computation, any degree of realism is possible as a setting for design. It may be simply blue sky, or it may be the entire urban setting for a project—the choice is the designer's.

Architectural plans are usually drawn with contour lines as a graphic indication of landform (Figure 8.1). Architects and contractors eventually become accustomed to this abstraction and can picture the form of the terrain from studying the contours, though it is certainly a learned skill. Common practice is to build a cardboard model of a building site that has any complexity. The model is made by cutting each contour line from cardboard and layering the sheets together into a three-dimensional visualization of the land. Contour lines drawn on a computer can be looked at in perspective to achieve a three-dimensional sense of the landform (Figure 8.2). With a complex building site this becomes an impressive display of the computer's mastery of perspective, producing a drawing that would virtually be impossible to achieve by hand.

Once the contour information has been put into the computer, color is an effective means for visually sculpting the landform. Use of a color ramp is a good technique for this. Figure 8.3 shows these same contours, but now rendered in color. The drawing uses a color ramp constructed in changing values of green. The darkest green is assigned to the lowest contour, the lightest green to the highest. Seen in per-

FIGURE 8.1.   Contour plan of a building site. (Graphic: John M. Young, Jr.)

spective, the line drawing has disappeared and a three-dimensional image of the terrain develops. The stepping of the landscape is highlighted by making the edge of each contour layer a lower saturation in order to articulate the mass of the land. It looks as if it is a cardboard model and can be looked at from innumerable points of view. These changes in value have made the shape of the land comprehensible to both layman and architect; they can become a base for a careful site analysis (Figure 8.4).

But no site is complete with just its contours; it also needs a collection of scale-giving elements to communicate the size of objects —to establish a sense of place. Buildings do this well, as do any objects

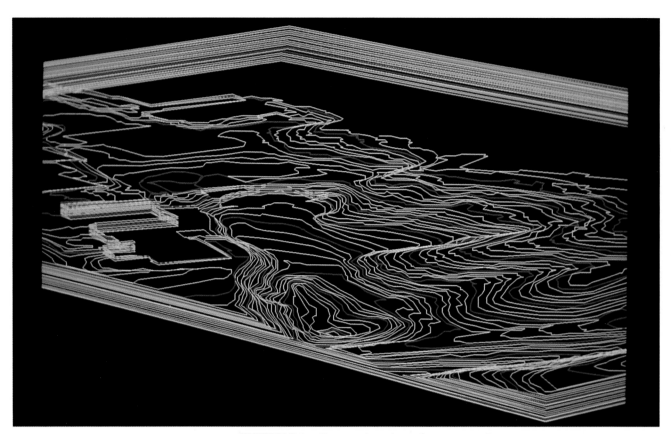

FIGURE 8.2.   Perspective view of a contour drawing. (Graphic: John M. Young, Jr.)

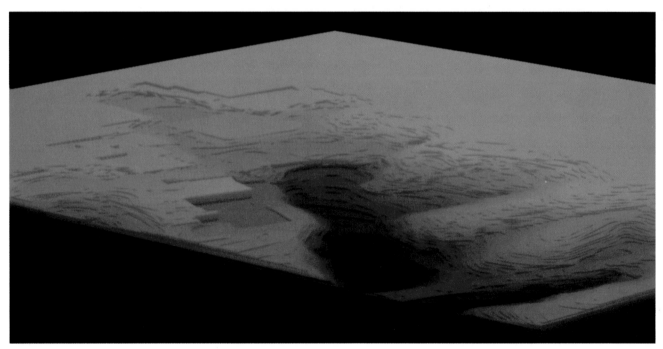

FIGURE 8.3.   Perspective view with contours in color. (Graphic: John M. Young, Jr.)

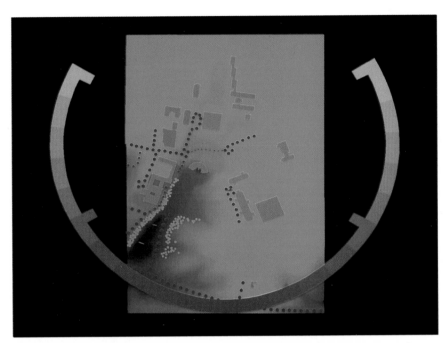

FIGURE 8.4.   Site plan rendered in color. (Graphic: John M. Young, Jr.)

of known size that give scale to a drawing. Color can be used to indicate the surrounding buildings, the tree forms, the circulation paths on the site, even the movement of the sun. Trees provide scale, and become a yardstick with which to measure the scope of a site.

The building program for a complex site can also become graphic when it is added to the computerized site. Color is useful in distinguishing between the parts of the building, helping to clarify its components. Figure 8.5 illustrates the building blocks of a program, with each element drawn to scale; its size is perceived relative to the site. The central entrance to this facility is drawn in magenta, selected as the complement of the green site in order to make it prominent. From this entrance, two functions are indicated, one in blue-purple and one in red-orange. Colors are selected to explain further the program, in this case developing a color ramp of hues—ramping from red, to magenta, to blue, and finally to purple, as an indication of programmatic relationships. This relationship is diagrammatically illustrated by the inclusion of a color wheel in the drawing.

Seen on the site, this programmatic information immediately gives an indication of building mass; it becomes a collection of shapes that can be manipulated and considered (Figure 8.6). As a designer you have more visual information before determining form and placement. While your decisions remain intuitive, your knowledge of both site and building require substantially less guesswork.

The computer provides a useful and flexible way to represent sites. For a simple first sketch, a background of green may be all that is appropriate. As a design progresses, the site may be more completely indicated. But whether simple or elaborate, the presentation of site information as planes of color will establish contrasts that make this information more readable and convey a comprehension of site to both client and professional.

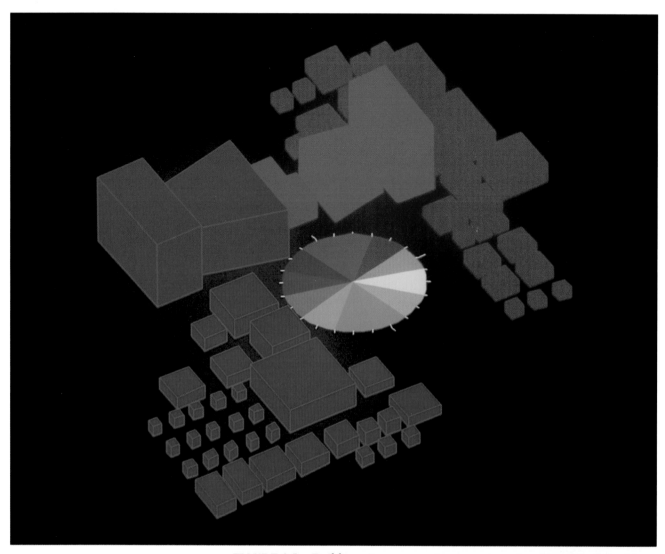

FIGURE 8.5.   Building site program in computer color. (Graphic: John M. Young, Jr.)

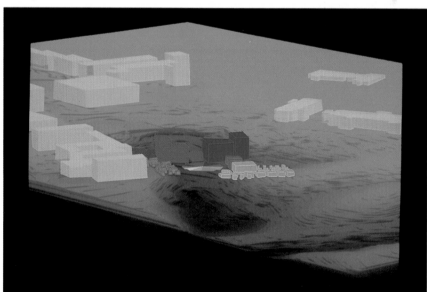

FIGURE 8.6.   A building program on its site. (Graphic: John M. Young, Jr.)

THE DESIGN OF BUILDINGS

An interesting phenomenon occurs in working with architectural color graphics. In the process of developing a design, there is a compulsion to move ever closer to color reality. The outcome of this tendency becomes a blurring of the distinction between design and presentation as drawings become more real. Computer drawings can simulate real world terms, and when they do there is less need to create drawings that simply "explain" a design. Traditional renderings and "final presentations" become less important in the practice of architecture if realism is achieved at each step in the developing design.

As the architect becomes more involved in color manipulation, color becomes a more natural part of the design process. Selecting the particular materials that compose a design could be done directly from the color drawings, automatically, for the material and its color have already been considered, and its specification is in the computer's memory.

In the real world, every building has a site that must be a part of the design deliberations. Site information must be entered into the computer, for the monitor does not provide context automatically. It is initially more empty than a drafting board—the black void of the picture tube is like space without stars, containing nothing except what is put there by the designer. It is an ideal place for the design of a space station (Figure 8.7), for in the clarity of this environment any object that is drawn will appear without clutter. By virtue of this emptiness, it is extremely responsive both to light and to a designer's intended coloration.

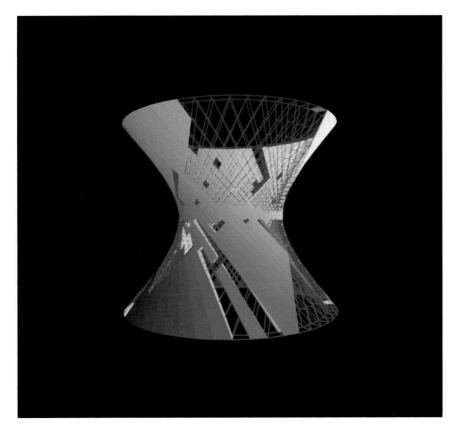

FIGURE 8.7. A space station.
(Graphic: John M. Young, Jr.)

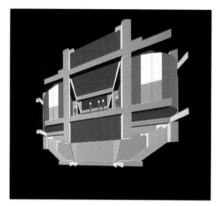

FIGURE 8.8.   Color study in space
—red. (Graphic: Charles A. Hardee)

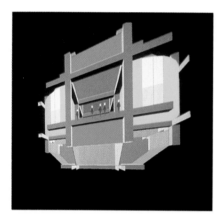

FIGURE 8.9.   Color study in space
—green.(Graphic: Charles A. Hardee)

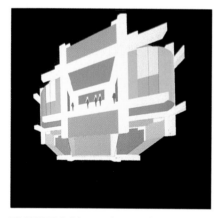

FIGURE 8.10.   Color study in space
—blue. (Graphic: Charles A. Hardee)

But the selection of colors is difficult for projects that have no context. The villa illustrated in Figures 8.8, 8.9, and 8.10, while carefully defined architecturally, has been colored in the void of the computer. The colors seem arbitrary; do you prefer the red, the green, or the blue? Without any suggestion of context, the only criteria for hue selection are the psychological preferences of the designer, or the dictates of fashion and taste.

The selection of color is a powerful means of relating a structure to its environment. Any locale has a coloration that contributes substantially to establishing the sense of place—it could be argued that regionalism is at least in part color-based. Environments have been created for the villas that are illustrated. One is placed in the desert

FIGURE 8.11.   Color study in context—red. (Graphic: Charles A. Hardee)

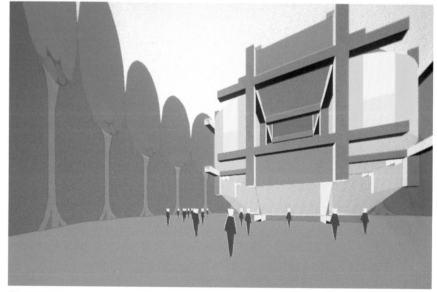

FIGURE 8.12.   Color study in context—green. (Graphic: Charles A. Hardee)

(Figure 8.11), another is a forest (Figure 8.12), and a third is on the beach (Figure 8.13). These are not detailed environments; if that were desired, a video camera image would work better. They are sketches of environments, designed to capture color and establish locale; the sort of drawing that could capture the essence of a place for a preliminary sketch. Technically a cyclorama screen of repeated scenic elements circles each villa—seen in plan it is a cylinder with a rudimentary landscape rendered on it that has been dropped around the villa. Coupled with a floor color and a ceiling color, these are adequate to establish context.

Colors for these villas have been selected to harmonize with their environments. This is probably not obvious in looking at them, for good color selection is often inconspicuous. But if you use some computer magic, it is simple to relocate each villa to the wrong setting (Figures 8.14, 8.15, 8.16). Now the villas are out of place—they are the wrong color for their environment. Often in choosing colors the negative illustration is useful in confirming the logic of a good selection. The availability of these color comparisons is one of the major advantages of computation.

The computer environment provides an ideal place to develop a building's coloration. In studying the elevation of a structure, color changes can be as simple to generate as changes in mass and proportion. In fact, the development of detailed massing can be produced along with the color specification. In Figures 8.17 and 8.18, two colorations are explored for the elevation of a building. While the image is not complex, it is adequate to provide a basis for color choice. The computer is suited to this developmental process; what is initially drawn as a simple mass of color becomes increasingly detailed as further design decisions are made.

Figure 8.19 is as much a study of color as it is of mass, a happy exploration of the two elements on the computer. Then, as the design for a building progresses, what initially was drawn as simple color mass can be articulated with considerable detail. The façade shown

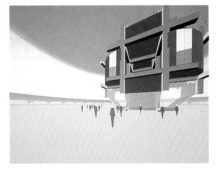

FIGURE 8.14.   Color study out of context—red. (Graphic: Charles A. Hardee)

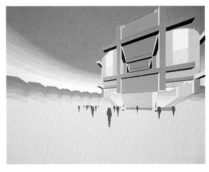

FIGURE 8.15.   Color study out of context—green. (Graphic: Charles A. Hardee)

FIGURE 8.16.   Color study out of context—blue. (Graphic: Charles A. Hardee)

FIGURE 8.13.   Color study in context—blue. (Graphic: Charles A. Hardee)

FIGURE 8.17.   Housing study in yellow. (Graphic: Matthew Rice)

FIGURE 8.18.   Housing study in red. (Graphic: Matthew Rice)

FIGURE 8.19.   Wonderwall.
(Graphic: Craig A. Gangloff)

FIGURE 8.20.   Façade. (Graphic:
Charles A. Hardee)

in Figure 8.20 indicates both detail and coloration; it is carefully considered in mass, proportion, and color. Each element contributes to the façade organization—each can be "processed" by computer. Colors for the facade have been chosen with care. The principal colors, gray and yellow, have been selected to give a three-dimensional quality; the yellow mass advances while the gray recedes. Because of these colors, the building appears less imposing on the street than if it were a solid, monolithic color. The minimal environment the computer provides should be noted in this illustration. A simple color ramp has been used to suggest the sky and to remove the drawing from the black context of the picture tube.

If one persists in the refinement of color modeling on the computer, then what begins as a simple design statement can become a very articulate image. Drawings in full color that illustrate with considerable realism both building and context become possible. For understanding one's own design, and for relating design information to a client, the computer is capable of producing drawings that far exceed traditional renderings in that they are able to communicate more design information. This is not a matter of rendering detail, for that can be done with traditional media. It is possible to interact with the computer drawing. The dynamic nature of the medium makes it possible not only to draw perspective, but to manipulate the perspective to indicate changing vantage points. The colors are dynamic in these drawings, and as an architect you can change materials, colors, or massing to respond to your own preferences or those of your client. The context is equally changeable, from day to night (Figures 5.22, 5.23) or from winter to summer. Because of the color imagery it produces, the computer presents a far more comprehensive image of the design.

As the complexity of a computer image grows, an astonishing amount of visual information can be accumulated. It is perhaps wise to interject a word of caution here, for there is still a gulf between theory and reality when it comes to computer drawing. Too much information can become burdensome. An overwhelming number of bits of graphic information can be produced, each of which must be entered into the computer, related to all the other information, and brought to the monitor screen in the right order to produce the desired images in the selected colors. There is a point that must be found by each designer, through experience and intuition, when the generation of further design information is not fruitful.

The high-rise building shown in Figure 8.21 is a wire-frame construction of a student entry for a design competition. Simple building masses have been constructed to indicate the urban context, and each floor of the project has been indicated as a line drawing. Color can add considerably to the comprehension of this drawing. When the polygons that form these lines are colored, the building becomes real in appearance and conveys design information more articulately (Figure 8.22). But considerably more design information must be recorded in order to accomplish this. The towers in the four corners of the building were conceived as glass-enclosed stairwells supported by a vertical truss of tubular steel. A detail of this is shown in Figure 8.23. Colors are selected in a ramp of value changes to suggest a rounding of the truss elements; stairs are sculpted to suggest shading; even the transparency of the glass wall is suggested through color changes. Piece by piece this information can be entered in the computer, for the repetition of design elements that characterize this building is well adapted to computer techniques. Each flight of stairs needs to be drawn only once and then repeated. As realistic as the results can be, the accumulated information involved is enormous (Figure 8.24), testing the computer's memory capacity as well as the value of such detail.

Design information is conveyed in these drawings with great beauty and clarity. As with any tool, however, judgment is required to determine when visual information is appropriate. Once you have seen the degree of detail that, through repetition and variation, it is possible to produce, detail can all too easily become a pursuit in itself. The value of a simple and changeable color drawing, one that uses color wisely to communicate design issues, should not be lost in the pursuit of architectural detail. In expressing the design of any building with computation, whether as simple sketches or as detailed drawings, the use of electronic color communicates information more clearly than is possible with traditional techniques.

FIGURE 8.21.   Urban high-rise, wire-frame drawing. (Graphic: John M. Young, Jr.)

FIGURE 8.22.   Urban high-rise, solid model drawing. (Graphic: John M. Young, Jr.)

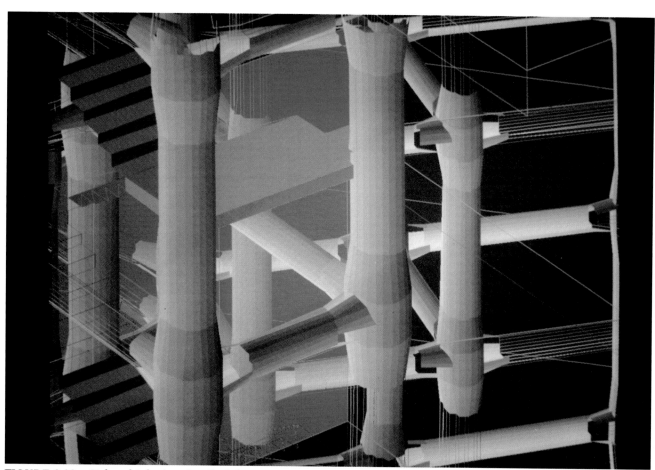

FIGURE 8.23.   Urban high-rise, detail of the stair tower. (Graphic: John M. Young, Jr.)

FIGURE 8.24.   Urban high-rise, detail of the building. (Graphic: John M. Young, Jr.)

THE COLOR OF CITIES

In Italy, considerable attention has been given to the color of cities. Northern Italian cities in particular are subject to being colored, for the local building tradition provides a heritage of homogeneous building masses, usually faced with stucco. This material is normally painted, and the color of the paint contributes substantially to the distinctive character of each urban center.

The color palette of Italian cities is different in each case, sometimes being left to the owner of a building, but more often conforming to local custom. The streets of Como, on the Swiss border, are dominated by the preferences of individual landlords, producing all manner of pastel colors that provide a degree of individual expression. Yet they are unified by a rather narrow range of value and saturation differences. These colors, when applied to buildings of similar scale and detail, produce a unified urban core.

In Genoa, on the Italian Riviera, vast areas of housing were built in the late nineteenth century. The stucco walls of the urban apartments are painted, rendered with painted-on windows and doors in the mannerist traditions that were popular in nineteenth-century Italy. The coloration of these buildings is fairly uniform, generated by an accepted palette of umbers and ochres that seem themselves to come from the Italian landscape. They are not unlike the color of the local soil.

Venice, with its unique environment of water, exhibits the most dynamic coloration of the Italian cities. The reflections of light and color that develop from its streets of water keep the building surfaces in constant change. These colors are mirrored in the water, animated by its ripples and waves (Marcolli 1988, 6.1). The characteristic color changes that Albers explored in defining transparency and depth seem to occur naturally as the waters of Venice change the color of the city over its daily cycle.

The computer provides an opportunity to coordinate urban coloration—only with the flexibility computation offers, could one hope to accommodate the dynamic, ever-changing nature of cities. A group in Torino, Italy, led by Giovanni Brino, envisioned large areas of their city colored in a coordinated manner and developed color proposals by computer. A palette was selected for the central city, each sample being identified with Munsell nomenclature and orchestrated through the city's streets and piazzas. A color plan for the central city was published, identifying colors that were distinct for each piazza (Figure 8.25). Drawing from the adjacent piazzas, a color recommendation was made for the buildings on connecting streets. Colors were proposed for a series of piazzas, each piazza unique in its color environment, each connected by boulevards, themselves unified in color (Brino 1982, 22).

The color mapping for cities that a computer makes possible opens opportunities for urban planning previously not conceivable. Whole boulevards were planned in Paris under the guidance of Baron Haussmann during the reign of Napoleon, boulevards that were unified in material and color by the use of a common building type and material. Today such planning, both for political reasons and due to the proliferation of building materials and types, is not conceivable, though the unity achieved by Haussmann's planning is much admired by architects and planners. Computers make it possible to establish color plans for cities and urban complexes. Such maps could record existing colors and register the changes that take place, projecting sequential color schemes for city squares and for streets that could both unify cities and provide diversity within them. The dynamic, changeable quality of a computer map would make this possible.

Figures 8.26 and 8.27 are alternative color plans for a housing development. Each map proposes color constants that unify the areas of the project, as well as suggesting zones that are distinguished by their color identities. Housing areas in American cities are extremely diverse in architectural expression and in color. They are in many ways the opposite of so many Italian streets where architectural unity is achieved in color and in form. Regulation is being brought to these subdivisions through zoning, through committees, and through the establishment of architectural review boards, but seldom is any effort being made to provide unity through control of color.

The elevations that are illustrated in figure 8.28 explore the effects of color on typical house forms. Elevations such as this, which indicate

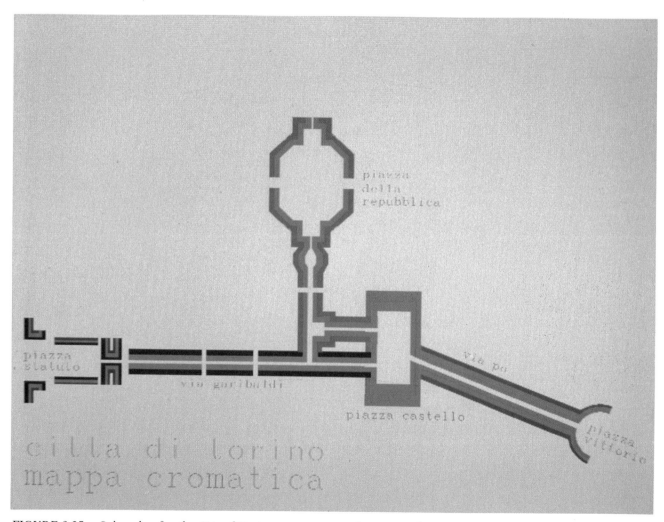

FIGURE 8.25.   Color plan for the City of Torino, a computer adaptation of the "Piano Regolatore Del Colore de Torino" by Giovanni Brino. (Graphic: the author)

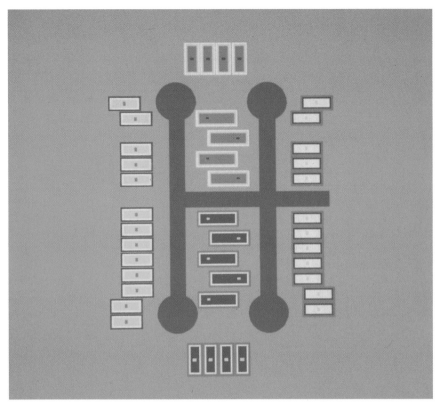

FIGURE 8.26.   Color plan for a housing development, scheme A. (Graphic: Gwinn Gibson Harvey and John M. Young, Jr.)

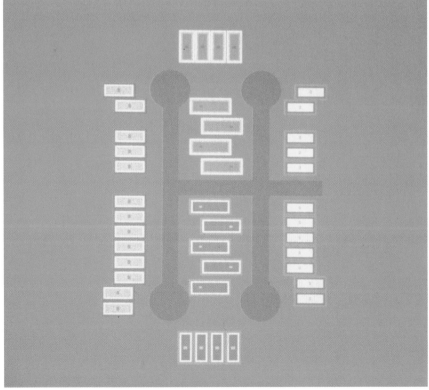

FIGURE 8.27.   Color plan for a housing development, scheme B. (Graphic: Gwinn Gibson Harvey and John M. Young, Jr.)

several housing units, could be developed from an approved color map. Through each group of houses runs a common coloration to unify the development, yet there is also an exploration of individual colors for the houses. Provision is made for both unity and variety through color selection. Housing developments lend themselves well to such coloration.

In Sweden, as in Japan, the construction of housing components is largely done by prefabrication in factories. The design of each house is personalized by discussions, over a computer, with the architect/manufacturer; components are selected and room arrangements developed to individualize each housing unit. The possibilities are enormous for relating these houses to a larger urban context through color processing by computer. Opportunities exist in our cities for imaginative coloration—for color designs that would unite disparate architectural elements and achieve a statement of community. The development of such approaches to color is one of the great opportunities of the computer generation.

FIGURE 8.28.   Color schemes for suburban housing. (Graphic: Clifford D. Kinard III)

EXERCISES

1. Design a building without context, a house in the black void of space. Now develop a color scheme for the house. What criteria have you used for color selection.
2. Draw the facade of a building in color. Now change the massing of that building by manipulating the colors of the facade.
3. Demonstrate the development of an architectural elevation. Use simple color shapes to sketch the preliminary massing; refine these areas into a careful color rendering of the facade.
4. Design a color plan for a project. Use color to bring both unity to the entire project and diversity to its parts.

REFERENCES

Brino, Giovanni. 1982. *Colore E Arredo Urbano Nei Centri Storici,* Secondo quaderno di L'Arredo Urbano e la Citta. Milano: Edizioni Over.

Marcolli, Attilio. 1988. *The Color Image.* Proceedings of the International Colour Association Symposium 1988. Winterthur, Switzerland: Colour Course Center, Winterthur Polytechnic.

Chapter 9

The Representation of Form

Y ou can use computation as a tool to access knowledge, to study ideas, or to present visual information. An amazing amount of information can be stored in a computer and kept ready and available. As a design tool, its potential is enormous. Designers have at their command both the total accumulation of architectural knowledge and all the tools needed for electronic visualization. By interacting with this knowledge base, designers become free to explore visual form and can immediately see the outcome of their ideas.

Such direct interaction between cause and effect is a powerful advantage that has not been possible in architecture. The availability of computation cannot help but alter the process of design itself. Traditional methods of conceiving buildings and producing documentation for construction is incredibly slow compared to the speed of electronic communication, and an impatient society increasingly will not wait for the old process to take place.

Television images influence everyone who sees them. We have all been profoundly changed by the television we watch, by the procession of spaces and the insight into places that it continuously models. And the popularity of TV is spreading; ideas, and images both good and bad, are communicated to the underdeveloped areas of the world with a rapidity heretofore inconceivable and are reshaping old cultures with new demands. In the Yucatan Peninsula, television sets are being installed in wattle and daub huts, creating a demand for cars and cosmetics where only dirt floors exist, proving again the power of the electronic image.

The computer image is similar to television in that it too is an electronic picture that can capture attention and give focus to view. If you become involved with computers, you soon discover that many hours can be passed in front of the computer screen. By interacting with a computer's images, you are able to participate in a dialog at whatever intellectual level you desire.

AUTOMATION OF THE CONSTRUCTION PROCESS

There is something inevitable about the automation of the construction industry. The same computers that are becoming design tools are also capable of moving robots. The time is not far away when any movement of the human body can be mimicked by a robot. These mechanical servants are now being used to weave carpets and to build cars; and they are beginning to enter the construction industry. In Japan it has been demonstrated that the steel frames of buildings can be completely assembled by robots; that concrete floors can be poured on these frames, and that the steel can be fireproofed—all without human intervention. Through experiments such as these, an expertise is being accumulated to build and train robots that mimic the construction process; soon machines will build buildings (Ohsaki 1987).

Robots are only mechanical hands and feet that are instructed in their every movement by computers. Once the design information needed to construct a building is in a computer, in theory it could be directed to robots. The potential exists for assembling buildings more efficiently with robotics than with construction workers. The information needed is all in the memory of computers; it is a stream of consciousness that begins with the conceptual design of a building and is developed, as the design is developed, with the identification of materials and appropriate methods of construction. Robots are the logical next step. It is not hard to visualize a world where buildings are designed using the computer, where building material manufacture is controlled by computer, and where materials are assembled into buildings by computer-directed robots. As one computer learns to speak with another, the process of construction becomes ever swifter, more accurate, and potentially more sensitive to the objectives of design.

There is nothing in this process that precludes the abilities of the individual; the capable and talented designer is in demand as never before. In fact, the complexity of information needed to design and assemble a large building automatically, by computer, is far more intense than the rather sketchy outline of information needed to handcraft a building. The very human process of assembling these facts can be aided by many facets of computer technology, but it is the designer, or more likely the team of designers, planners, engineers, and builders that will control this process.

You may rightly ask what color has to do with an automated design process. Color is at its very heart, for the visualization of an emerging design that is afforded by color composition is what will enable the design team to predict and understand every facet of the extended design process necessary for automation. Computers must communicate design information to the people who control them and their clients, with clarity and with accuracy. Electronically colored images can provide the clarity of visual information this process needs.

Careful and knowing manipulation of color is central to an extended design process. It is by the judicious selection of color that forms are defined, forms that through the process of design will become materials and eventually buildings. Color selection begins with the initial definition of space and form; it can continue as a design is developed in detail and as materials are selected and shaped to form building and cities.

Specification of the color of building components can also be achieved by computer. It is being done in the textile industry now. Clothing is designed and colored by computer—moving from the designer's image on the screen directly to the selection of warp and woof in the mill. An automated construction industry cannot wait for the composition of an after-the-fact color board to define a project's coloration. It is in fact unreasonable for a designer to postpone this design decision until everything else has been decided. Color, as a component of the design, can be chosen like any essential ingredient. Its selection should parallel the definition of the form, space, and texture that constitute the design. Color should be specified along with materials and methods of construction. And as with other components of the design, color could be specified by computer.

Computation can be used to provide a complete and integrated visualization of any design proposal. By achieving these visualizations with electronic color, clearer images can be produced and better communication achieved, providing an opportunity to bring the design to a more successful fruition.

In this process there is no diminution of the designer's role; it is in fact increased, as every facet of the design becomes committed to the computer prior to the beginning of construction. In order to achieve successful automation of the construction process, an abundance of design information must be communicated with rapidity and thoroughness, and color provides that communication.

INTUITION IN DRAWING

Design has always been intuitive; designers are forced to move between known facts and their own intuitive judgments. A successful design is rich in both assembled fact and in the assumptions that develop intuitively as a part of the process. Computation can assist this intuition as a tool for visualization. Most CAAD and computer drawing programs have been written with this goal.

To be useful to you as a designer of buildings, a computer program should not burden you with any of the preconceptions or the methodologies of the computer programmer, though this ideal has proved difficult to achieve. Many computer systems, for example, will design a typical modern office building—a rectangular proportion of proper dimensions; a central core to handle stairs, toilets, and elevators; a thin skinned, well-proportioned exterior wall; all arranged at a height and size to fit a particular set of needs—this can be achieved without any problem on the computer. But if you want to rethink the problem of the office building, as Frank Lloyd Wright did when he designed the Larkin Building in Buffalo, as Gordon Bunshaft did with the Lever Building, or as Le Corbusier did at Chandigarh; then—to be computer-aided—you must find a more generic tool for computation. You must return to the basic building blocks of form and examine once again the elements of design—the lines, shapes, spaces, and colors that are the substance of every architectural composition.

These elements are an essential part of most computer programs for architecture. The manipulation of "line" is an efficient and ac-cepted means of computer drawing. The description of both "form" and "space" is becoming commonplace. Orthographic drawing with lines is common, and the mathematics of perspective is being rapidly incorporated into these programs as memory capacity is expanded. The availability of an extensive color palette opens even richer possi-bilities for the support of conceptual design on the computer. Color is able to enhance intuitive judgment through the imagery it provides. By using contrasting colors, you can communicate better your intui-tive judgments about form. There is no vision, no imagery, without the contrast of color to define it. Line drawings of forms are but illu-sions of those forms, definitions of color boundaries, unless they are filled with the hues, the values, and the saturations that will make them speak one to another.

The first drawings of buildings make extremely interesting stud-ies, for they are highly intuitive; often they are more figments of the imagination rather than a depiction of form. The sketches of Le Cor-busier are probably best known to design students, for they have been often published; usually such drawings are lost as they become quickly superseded by more developed drawings.

The first drawings of Frank Lloyd Wright are equally intuitive. The sketches for the Larkin Building, for example, suggest the formal massing of the building. These sketches are more illusion than im-agery. They are a manifestation of the designer's imagination, drawn from something seen, something thought, or something remembered, and drawn in the most expedient manner. They will eventually define a massing for the buildings involved, but initially they are only searches for appropriate form. Because of the available tools, such drawings have generally been drawn as line drawings.

When the computer makes color accessible as a tool for sketching, then computation contributes substantially to the conceptualization of architecture, enhancing the designer's intuitive judgment through color images. A line drawing is not a natural impression of form, something that relates to everyday vision. It is a learned technique, a delineation of the boundaries of color. Through experience we come to read the lines of sketches as color boundaries, but line drawings are really abstractions we have been conditioned to accept. Turn back to the comparison of wire-frame drawing and color drawing (Figures 2.1 and 2.2), shown in Chapter 2. Who would not prefer the color drawing? Who would not find that through color, a designer is able to convey more completely the intent of the design? If through computation designers were given an opportunity to communicate their intentions both quickly and in color, they would have a new tool that would improve the process of architectural design.

Sketches in color communicate design information well. When drawn with colored imagery, the intent of any design is made clearer to the designer and to anyone looking at the design. We are not talking about exactness here, for there is considerable merit to be found in the ambiguity of a design sketch. Color drawings too can be vague in intent. But even through a mask of ambiguity, the implications of form and of the space are made clearer through use of color.

Color sketches are capable of conveying considerable emotional content; the psychological reaction to the colors used in sketches can be very powerful. In an architect's first sketches for a project, the colors can be far more intense in saturation and contrasting in value than would be acceptable in the built environment. Their psychological impact is enhanced. An ability to exaggerate the emotional content of a sketch is highly desirable when there is no further information to detail an idea. At that point there is so little known and so much implied. Any tool that permits the designer to express undeveloped intent is both powerful and useful. As an aid to intuition, the color sketch may be unsurpassed.

INTUITION IN DESIGN

The work of Thomas Jefferson, probably the best known of early American designers, can provide a unique illustration of the traditional role that intuition has played in design. Jefferson today is respected as both statesman and architect. The architecture for which he is remembered, the campus of the University of Virginia and his own home at Monticello, are among the most enduring of America's architectural landmarks. They represent a sort of American ideal in architectural design, highly creative concepts, endowed with individuality and conforming to the best of eighteenth-century architectural scholarship. They are informed, yet intuitive in concept.

Jefferson's home at Monticello was strongly influenced by the designs of Palladio. Probably because of his familiarity with Palladian concepts, Jefferson's Monticello is very different from the traditional American homestead. Normally in a rural development the first house would be located near a source of water, on a stream or river, and outbuildings would appear in a random manner as needs developed. Jefferson proposed, and over his lifetime created, a unified formal design for an entire rural agricultural complex. His design is formal in concept and axial in execution, as a proper Palladian building should be; it provides hierarchy of spaces for both landholder and slave, for implement and larder, all within a formal arrangement of space (McLaughlin 1988).

The Jeffersonian concept is in principle what one finds in touring the surviving works of Palladio in the Italian countryside. One sees large agrarian complexes with a symmetrical ordering—farmhouse and related buildings arranged in a holistic design statement. But the arrangement of space at Monticello, its adaptation to its site in the forested lands of the American Blue Ridge, and its location on top of the hill is uniquely the creation of Thomas Jefferson. There is little in Palladio to suggest the layering of spaces into the Virginia hillside that Jefferson has achieved. While respecting and learning from precedent, Monticello was born of Jefferson's imagination as a young man and nurtured by his maturing judgment. Backed with scholarship and a strong sense of propriety, the design of site and building at Monticello was *intuitive*.

Jefferson's concept is clearly drawn from an assemblage of fact. There were, for example, all the functions of a rural, postcolonial estate to consider to create a self-sustaining community of several hundred people. To support this, a substantial agricultural hinterland was required. A clothing industry to supply the needs of both slave and master was needed, and a building industry to manufacture the greater portion of the architecture. The many guests who visited the Jeffersons were in need of accommodations; rooms were required that spoke well of Jefferson's position of leadership in the young country. Then there were his personal needs to be satisfied: space for a library, spaces in which to entertain friends, but also spaces to meet his need for privacy and retreat.

In his role as a national political figure, Jefferson was well read and well traveled. His personal library contained many books on architecture, including the plan books that were an accepted source eighteenth-century architectural education, and an extensive library of the broad general reading on architecture expected of a man of letters. Among these are to be found the literature and drawings of Andrea Palladio, the Italian architect widely admired in both England and America and a respected source from which to learn. To this collection of literature one must add the travels Jefferson undertook. As a statesman, he visited most of the cities in the former colonies; as American Ambassador to France, he lived for several years in Paris, giving him the opportunity to study the architecture of that city and to explore the architecture of Europe. While in Europe, he collected a good deal of architectural literature. As a scholar, Jefferson was versed in the best current methods of architectural problem solving. As an architect, he was well prepared to design Monticello (McLaughlin 1988).

The architectural "program" for Monticello is long and involved. Were it to be written today as a computerized program statement, it would be a formidable list of functions and desires. As ludicrous as it is to suggest for a moment that a computer could have achieved a successful design for Monticello, certainly the architectural program for the Monticello complex could have been more explicit had it been carefully annotated by computer. Many details would have to be borne in mind. One could say with reasonable certainty that the quantities of food required to sustain the complex would be more accurately predicted using a computer, and specification of storage requirements would be more exacting. Probably the number of bedrooms required in the house could be predicted with greater accuracy, and surely a functional analysis would produce a clearer circulation pattern through the house.

It could also be said that the construction, which occupied the greater portion of Jefferson's lifetime, would have been more efficient had someone listed all the factors involved: the interruptions, those shortages of both supplies and labor, and at times the shortage of construction funds. With a well-articulated critical path diagram, one might have found a more direct and economical sequence of construction. By careful manipulation of money flow in relation to anticipated building costs, construction time might have been shortened and costs lessened for the entire project.

Conceptual design, however, the outstanding achievement at Monticello, is a very different matter. Could the computer have assisted in the visual imagery of Monticello? Would Jefferson's intuitive judgments have been better given a more thorough drawing tool? Figure 9.1 is a computer rendering of Monticello as it stands today, an image far beyond what Jefferson could produce.

Now there is discussion of the development of "automatic problem solvers" for design, software that uses the computer to achieve an

FIGURE 9.1.   Thomas Jefferson's home at Monticello. (Computer graphic design by Gary Bodine, student, School of Architecture/N.J.I.T.)

automated design process. The order that Palladian design brings to architecture might be an interesting beginning for such a program. The formal order so evident in Palladian buildings, the division of a central mass into subordinate parts, are all design ideas that might be codified. The axial and symmetric extension of space to accommodate a given program, such as that of Monticello, might be submitted to mathematical structuring. The hierarchy of space that structures the Palladian buildings is probably a programmable commodity; one need only prioritize the programmed areas.

But the concept of Monticello, the selection of its mountaintop site with its unique adaptation to landform, was certainly and properly an intuitive decision. The biased arrangement of architectural spaces, the deliberate expression of democracy and equality within the plan of the house, are all the result of intuitive judgments by the architect.

This intuition must be cherished and nurtured, for it is this portion of the design process that is the unique contribution of the architect as an individual. It is through intuitive judgment that the dreams of ambitious people are realized, and that the best and most enduring architecture is usually achieved.

Computation can provide all the information needed for intuitive judgment in a readily accessible form on the screen; the sorting and cataloging of this information is probably best left to computers, for they are proven workhorses in this regard. But once a conceptual design is achieved, computation can support that design through computer drawing procedures that are becoming standard in architectural practice. As any design develops, there is a continuing need for intuitive judgment, and this is the proper role of a designer.

In the time between the initial analysis of a design problem and that moment when a building's first commitment is made to drawing, an intuitive judgment is made (Norman 1987, 296). At this point, through intuition, the designer determines a form for the building. This single point of creativity is the most evasive portion of an otherwise definable, quantifiable design process. It defies analysis and therefore it defies computation.

As a designer, it is fitting and proper that you make the intuitive decisions, for you alone have all the information at hand. You understand the needs as well as the intent of your client, or your patron; you have all this information well tabulated and at your fingertips; as a designer you can bring together a lifetime of experience and ambition, and apply these to develop a concept for a design.

While the design of Monticello is rich in its architectural outcome, the process of achieving it was both laborious and time-consuming. Thomas Jefferson possessed the intellect of an outstanding architect; he had the spirit of a builder and the understanding of space and form that is necessary to good design. He had an excellent comprehension of the social order he lived in and was intellectually capable of making a design response to it. But the tools with which he worked were by today's standards woefully inadequate.

Intuitive judgment cannot be computed. Given better tools, the architectural concepts that intrigued Jefferson could be more easily studied, understood, and manipulated by their creator and conveyed as information to others. Color can aid that intuition as it is used to both define form and to express the spirit of form.

FORM AND COLOR

To see a form is to experience color, for it is color that conveys to the eye an image of the form that has been seen—this rather simplistic observation is at the root of our perception. Form *is* color, color *is* form. Without color, any form is indistinguishable from its surroundings; it has no definition. Objects are modeled with color, modeled by the shades and shadows of their surfaces, modeled by the color differences that distinguish them from their environment.

The artists of the Bauhaus were well aware of the relationship of form to color. They taught that form and color were different manifestations of the same phenomenon. Josef Albers is quoted as saying: "Without colour there is no form. Form and colour are one. The colours of the spectrum are those most easily comprehended. Every possible colour lies dormant in them" (Whitford 1984, 106). These artists promoted the commonality of form and color in their teaching and their art; hence the well-known red square, blue circle, and yellow triangle. While not everyone has agreed with the literal interpretation of this Bauhaus dictum, there does appear to be an inseparable bond between form and color.

Writing many years earlier, Goethe was aware of the interrelationship between form and color. As an epilogue to his color theory, he says:

> The Eye sees no forms. It only sees that which differentiates itself through light and dark or through color.
>
> In the infinitely delicate sensibility for shade-graduation of light and dark as well as color lies the possibility of painting.
>
> Painting is truer to the eye than reality itself. It creates what man should see and wishes to see and not what he usually does see.
>
> The sensibility for forms, particularly beautiful forms, rests much deeper.
>
> The enjoyment of colors, individually or in harmony, is experienced by the eye as an organ, and it communicates its pleasure to the rest of the man. The enjoyment of form rests in man's higher nature, and is communicated by the inner man to the eye (Goethe, 1971, 197).

Karl Gerstner, in his book *The Forms of Color*, has said: "Form is the body of color and color the soul of form" (Gerstner 1986, 8). As a sculptor, Gerstner has emphatically pursued the relationship of pure form to pure color. In a study that seems a continuation of the work of Goethe and Kandinsky on the relationship of form to color, he goes on to say:

> Each individual color has its own character, which distinguishes it from all other colors. The difference may be minimal and barely perceptible or intensified to the point of contrariety: light-dark, pure-impure, color-complementary.
>
> The same is also true—with different parameters—of forms. The relationship in which the various colors, or forms, stand to each other produces interaction.
>
> There are not only interactions on the one hand between colors and, on the other, between forms but also between colors and forms. No color is conceivable without form and no form without color. Conversely, any color can be pictured in any form and any form in any color. Form is the body of color and color the soul of form (Gerstner 1986, 8).

What Karl Gerstner has so poetically stated is what has finally been realized by most individuals who have pursued, for one reason or another, the study of color: that there exists a mutual bond between a form and its color that is inseparable. Through the use of electronic color, we can maximize this bond. We can use computation to display, to select or reject colors, and ultimately to produce with color the images of form and space that best define our creative efforts.

EXERCISES

1. Explore your own composition of red squares, yellow triangles, and blue circles; is there validity today in this Bauhaus-defined relationship?
2. What is the form of green?

REFERENCES

Albers, Josef. 1963. *Interaction of Color.* New Haven, CT: Yale University Press.

Gerstner, Karl. 1986. *The Forms of Color.* Cambridge, MA: The MIT Press.

Goethe, Johann Wolfgang von. 1971 [1829]. *Goethe's "Color theory."* Arr. and ed. Rupprecht Matthaei. New York: Van Nostrand Reinhold.

McLaughlin, Jack. 1988. *Jefferson and Monticello, the Biography of a Builder.* New York: Henry Holt and Company.

Norman, Richard, 1987. Intuitive design and computation. In *Principles of Computer-Aided Design: Computability of Design,* ed. Yehuda E. Kalay, pp. 295–301. New York: Wiley.

Ohsaki, Yorihiko. 1987. Paper read at Annual Research Conference of the AIA/ACSA Council on Architectural Research, 18–20 November, World Trade Center, Boston.

Bibliography

Albers, Josef . 1963. *Interaction of Color,* New Haven, CT: Yale University Press.

Boll, Harold. 1986. The role of a color space in computer aided design. Paper read at Clemson University Computer Color Graphics Conference, 8–9 April, Greenville, SC.

Brino, Giovanni. 1982. *Colore E Arredo Urbano Nei Centri Storici,* Secondo quaderno di L'Arredo Urbano e la Citta. Milano: Edizioni Over.

Cohen, Michael F. 1987. Radiosity based lighting design. In *Computability of Design,* ed. Yehuda E. Kaley, pp. 303–313. New York: Wiley.

Fisher, Thomas, and Vernon Mays. 1988. The maturing micro. *Progressive Architecture* 69(4):126–31.

Goethe, Johann Wolfgang von. 1971 (1829). *Goethe's "Color theory."* Arr. and ed. Rupprecht Matthaei, trans. Herb Aach. New York: Van Nostrand Reinhold.

Gerstner, Karl. 1986. *The Forms of Color.* Cambridge, MA: The MIT Press.

Gerritsen, Frans. 1975. *Theory and Practice of Color.* New York: Van Nostrand Reinhold.

Gerritsen, Frans. 1988. *Evolution in Color.* West Chester, PA: Schiffer Publishing.

Greenberg, Donald P. 1989. Light reflection models for computer graphics. *Science* 244:166–173.

Itten, Johannes. 1973 [1961]. *The Art of Color: The Subjective Experience and Objective Rationale of Color.* Trans. Ernst van Haagen. New York: Van Nostrand Reinhold.

Koos, Uwe. 1982. *Basic Introduction to Color Design.* STO AG Stuhlingen, W. Germany: STO-Design Studio (Color Area Space), STO Systems Technology Organization.

Marcolli, Attilio. 1988. *The Color Image.* Proceedings of the International Colour Association Symposium 1988. Winterthur, Switzerland: Colour Course Center, Winterthur Polytechnic.

Matthaei, Rupprecht, ed. 1971. *Goethe's Color Theory.* American ed. New York: Van Nostrand Reinhold.

McLaughlin, Jack, 1988. *Jefferson and Monticello: The Biography of a Builder.* New York: Henry Holt and Company.

McLuhan, Marshall. 1967. *The Medium Is the Massage.* New York: Bantam Books.

Mitchell, William J., Robin S. Liggett, and Thomas Kvan. 1987. *The Art of Computer Graphics Programming.* New York: Van Nostrand Reinhold.

Munsell, Albert. 1976 [1924]. *The Munsell Book of Color.* Baltimore: Munsell Color Company, Inc.

Munsell, Albert. 1969. *A Grammar of Color: A Basic Treatise on the Color System of Albert H. Munsell.* Ed. and with an introd. by Faber Birren. New York: Van Nostrand Reinhold.

Norman, Richard. 1987. Intuitive design and computation. In *Principles of Computer-Aided Design: Computability of Design,* ed. Yehuda E. Kalay, pp. 295–301. New York: Wiley.

Ohsaki, Yorihiko. 1987. Paper read at Annual Research Conference of the AIA/ACSA Council on Architectural Research, 18–20 November, World Trade Center, Boston.

Poling, Clark V. 1986. *Kandinsky's Teaching at the Bauhaus: Color Theory and Analytical Drawing.* New York: Rizzoli International Publications, Inc.

Simon, Frederick T. 1986. Introduction to accurate representation of surface colors through color graphics. Paper read at Clemson University Computer Color Graphics Conference, 8–9 April, Greenville, SC.

Sullivan, Louis H. 1947. Ornament in architecture. In *Kindergarten Chats (revised 1918) and Other Writings.* Originally published in *The Engineering Magazine,* August 1892.

Taylor, Joann M., Gerald M. Murch, and Paul A. McManus. 1988. Tektronix HVC: A uniform perceptual color system for display users. Tektronix Laboratories, Beaverton, OR. *S.I.D. Digest* (Society for Information Display), May 24–26, 77–80.

Verity, Enid. 1980. *Color Observed.* New York: Van Nostrand Reinhold.

Weber, Nicholas Fox. 1988. The artist as alchemist. In *Josef Albers: A Retrospective.* New York: Solomon R. Guggenheim Museum.

Whitford, Frank. 1984. *Bauhaus.* London: Thames and Hudson.

Index